START YOUR OWN

CONSTRUCTION AND CONTRACTING BUSINESS

Additional titles in Entrepreneur's Startup Series

Start Your Own

Arts and Crafts Business

Automobile Detailing Business

Bar and Club

Bed and Breakfast

Blogging Business

Business on eBay

Car Wash

Child-Care Service

Cleaning Service

Clothing Store and More

Coaching Business

Coin-Operated Laundry

College Planning Consultant Business

Construction and Contracting Business

Consulting Business

Day Spa and More

eBusiness

eLearning or Training Business

Event Planning Business

Executive Recruiting Business

Fashion Accessories Business

Florist Shop and Other Floral Businesses

Food Truck Business

Freelance Writing Business and More

Freight Brokerage Business

Gift Basket Business and More

Grant-Writing Business

Graphic Design Business

Green Business

Hair Salon and Day Spa

Home Inspection Service

Import/Export Business

Information Marketing Business

Kid-Focused Business

Lawn Care or Landscaping Business

Mail Order Business

Medical Claims Billing Service

Microbrewery, Distillery, or Cidery

Net Services Business

Nonprofit Organization

Online Coupon or Daily Deal Business

Online Education Business

Personal Concierge Service

Personal Training Business

Pet Business and More

Pet-Sitting Business and More

Photography Business

Public Relations Business

Restaurant and More

Retail Business and More

Self-Publishing Business

Seminar Production Business

Senior Services Business

Specialty Food Businesses

Staffing Service

Transportation Service

Travel Business and More

Tutoring and Test Prep Business

Vending Business

Wedding Consultant Business

Wholesale Distribution Business

Entrepreneur
MAGAZINE'S

::i STARTUP

START YOUR OWN

CONSTRUCTION AND CONTRACTING BUSINESS

Third Edition

YOUR STEP-BY-STEP GUIDE TO SUCCESS

The Staff of Entrepreneur Media, Inc. & Rich Mintzer

Entrepreneur
PRESS®

Entrepreneur Press, Publisher
Cover Design: Andrew Welyczko
Production and Composition: Eliot House Productions

This publication is designed to provide accurate and authoritative information in regard to the
subject matter covered. It is sold with the understanding that the publisher is not engaged in
rendering legal, accounting or other professional services. If legal advice or other expert assistance
is required, the services of a competent professional person should be sought.

Library of Congress Cataloging-in-Publication Data
  Names: Mintzer, Richard, author. | Kuehn, Gregg. Start your own construction and contracting
    business. | Entrepreneur Press, publisher.
  Title: Start your own construction and contracting business : your step-by-step guide to success
    / The Staff of Entrepreneur Media, Inc. and Rich Mintzer.
  Description: Third Edition. | Irvine : Entrepreneur Press, 2016. | Series: Startup series | Revised
    edition of Start your own construction and contracting business, 2013.
  Identifiers: LCCN 2016007151| ISBN 978-1-59918-591-0 (paperback) | ISBN 1-59918-591-1
  Subjects: LCSH: Construction industry. | Contractors' operations. | New business enterprises. |
    BISAC: BUSINESS & ECONOMICS / Entrepreneurship.
  Classification: LCC HD9715.A2 M446 2016 | DDC 624.068/1—dc23
  LC record available at https://lccn.loc.gov/2016007151

Printed in the United States of America

20 19 18 17 16   10 9 8 7 6 5 4 3 2 1

Contents

Preface xi

Chapter 1
The Contracting Industry 1
   The Players 3
   Economic Importance. 5
   Wrap-Up 6

Chapter 2
Why Become a Contractor? 7
   Contractors Are Important to Their Communities . . .8
   Do You Have What It Takes?—Part I 9
      Do You Have the Proper Background? 10
      Formal Education 11
      On-the-Job Training (OJT) 11
      Lloyd Price. 12
      Discipline and Determination 12
      Self-Confidence 13
      Good Health 13

Excellent Time Management Skills 13
Do You Have What It Takes?—Part II 14
Continuing Education 15
Tools 16
Learn the Lingo. 17
Money Issues 17
Management Expertise 19
Wrap-Up 22

Chapter 3

The Business Plan 25

Business Plan Software 29
Mission Statement 30
Financing Your Business. 30
Venture Capitalists 30
Angel Investors 31
Debt Financing. 31
Credit Unions 32
Small Business Association 32
Wrap-Up 33

Chapter 4

Law and the G-Man 35

Business Structure 36
Accounting Methods. 38
Bankers, Lawyers, Accountants,
and Insurance Agents 39
Coping with the Government 40
Employees or Subcontractors. 42
Employee Benefits 42
Health Plans Can Offer Tremendous Benefits 43
Documentation and Receipts. 43
Wrap-Up 45

Chapter 5

It's Moving Day 47

Open Your Office and Shop. 48
Space: The Next Frontier 49
Office Specifications and Details. 50

Communications I 50
Communications II 51
Communications III. 52
Computers. 52
Office Supplies 53
Tools and Equipment. 55
The Bureaucracy. 55
Credit Cards 56
Supplier Credit 56
Banking 57
Start Me Up. 57
'Tis the Season 60
Wrap-Up 60

Chapter 6
Financial Techniques for Profitability 63

The Tools to Make a Budget. 64
Accounting Tools. 65
Why Set a Budget?. 66
Costs First. 66
Direct Costs. 67
Fixed Costs 72
Variable Costs 75
Overhead 77
Break-Even Point 80
Budget Overview. 80
Preparing the Estimate 80
Profits: The Bottom Line 83
Wrap-Up 86

Chapter 7
Contribution Margin and the Impact on Profits 87

How to Calculate Contribution Margin. 88
The Doctor Is In. 91
Wrap-Up 95

Chapter 8
Promoting Your Services 97

Get Your Website up Immediately 98

Web Layout and Design.................................100
Establishing an Online Presence 101
Self-Promotion 102
Demographics.....................................103
Print It! 103
Word of Mouth 105
Too Much of a Good Thing? 106
Wrap-Up 107

Chapter 9
Get a Job....................................109
The Employee Handbook..............................110
Applications and Hiring Forms.........................111
Job Descriptions...................................111
Minors Are Major 112
Wages and Benefits 112
Turnover 115
Organizational Chart................................116
Wrap-Up 118

Chapter 10
Errors and Omissions 119
Failure Is Not an Option..............................120
Client Complaints 121
The Nightmare Client................................123
How to Handle Client Complaints 124
Reliable Suppliers..................................125
Know the Enemy 126
Hiring Subcontractors................................127
Wrap-Up 128

Chapter 11
PANIC Is Proper..............................129
When to PANIC....................................130
Let's PANIC Now...................................130
P Is for Perseverance 130
A Is for Accounting 131
N Is for Natural Ability 131
I Is for Instinct....................................133

C Is for Communication 133
But, What If . . .? 134
Put Me in, Coach 134
The Beginning 135

Appendix
Construction Contracting Resources **137**

Books 138
Construction, Remodeling, and
General Contractor Magazine Websites 138
LinkedIn (www.linkedin.com) Group 139
Government Resources 139
General Business Websites 139
Cellphone Information 139
Contractor Resources 140
Listings and Places to Post Your Services 140
Accounting Software 140
Find Your Credit Rating 140
Credit Rating Bureaus 140
Education/Industry Links 141
Architecture 141
Engineering 141
Construction Industry Associations 141
Information and Tools 142
Social Media 142
Social Media Management 142

Glossary **143**

Index **147**

Preface

There's an old story about two men who drive up to a residential property in an unmarked rusty van, knock on the front door, and inform the homeowner that they can reseal the owner's cracked asphalt driveway at only a little more than half the going rate. The homeowner, Mr. Jones, strapped for cash after taking his family on a theme-park vacation, readily agrees to pay cash for the work. The next day, three men arrive bright and early, sweep dirt and leaves off the driveway, and proceed to apply a thin black substance to the driveway. They finish the job quickly and place protective yellow ribbon around the driveway.

After packing their tools in the van, they show Mr. Jones the finished project, telling him not to walk or drive on the asphalt for two days in order to give the sealer plenty of time to harden. "You don't wanna track the black stuff into your house," they inform him.

Delighted to have saved money and have the job finished quickly, Mr. Jones readily pays cash for the job. He's so happy with the results, he forgets to get a receipt. The only thing he knows is that the lead man's name is "Joe."

Very early the next morning, while Mr. Jones is dreaming about his golf game scheduled for that day, a wild and thunderous rainstorm awakens him and his wife. Trees bend in the storm, small branches break, and their rain gutters overflow. They give up their sleep and plod to the kitchen for their morning coffee.

Mr. Jones steps outside as dawn is breaking to retrieve the morning newspaper that is usually tossed onto his driveway. He takes a few steps and is dumbstruck by what he sees. His driveway is no longer black. The old cracks are still evident and even more prominent because of the rain. But his lawn is black and the gutter along the street is full of black goo. The light bulb goes on as Mr. Jones realizes that he has been taken. The men did not seal his driveway yesterday—they just "painted" it with some sort of black liquid.

Weeks later, after paying more than the going rate for a proper sealing job and additional money to have a portion of his lawn reseeded, Mr. Jones comes to the realization that he will either have to give up his weekly game of golf or tell the family that there will be no vacation next summer.

You've all heard such stories about inept, incompetent, inefficient, and sometimes downright crooked contractors. There are websites dedicated to contractor horror stories, TV news magazine shows that highlight unscrupulous contractors, and organizations like the Better Business Bureau that monitor the activities of problem companies.

So in these circumstances, why in the world would anyone want to start his or her own contracting business? Fortunately, the vast majority of contractors are honest, hard-working folks who provide valuable services to the general public. They are talented men and women who have a positive vision of the future and a burning desire to use their talents for the betterment of not only themselves and their families but also for their community and fellow citizens.

This book covers many facets of the contracting business: It includes checklists for getting started, ideas on marketing your services, and guidelines on how to price these services to make a reasonable profit. It presents ideas for hiring and managing employees and what to do when something goes wrong, either with those employees or with your customers. Along the way we'll include valuable tips, statistics, and facts about running your own business.

The goal is simple: We want you to know how to start your contracting business and keep it running smoothly, efficiently, and profitably.

1

The
Contracting
Industry

The contracting industry is both huge and varied. All sorts of people and companies call themselves contractors. On one side of the coin are thousands of profiteering contractors who made money off the war in Iraq, who supplied Americans on the front lines with everything from meals, laundry, and housing, to drivers, translators, bodyguards, and garbage collectors.

We also know of the hard-working and talented contractors who were instrumental in making the Apollo missions to the moon such a huge success.

These are examples of the far edges of the contracting industry: major companies with thousands of contract employees at one end of the spectrum and the individual specialist on the other end.

The intent of this book is to provide knowledge to either individual entrepreneurs or to small teams of entrepreneurs who want to start businesses providing contracting services to other businesses or individuals involved in property development. These contractors may provide services to individual homeowners; developers of apartment, condominium, or commercial complexes; governments who develop public parks, plazas, and other recreational areas; or developers of residential subdivisions and housing developments.

stat fact

According to the Small Business Administration, approximately 10 to 12 percent of businesses open and 10 to 12 percent of businesses close each year. About half of those that open survive for five years; only one-third are still operating after ten years.

In simple terms, there are two types of contractors who work with property development. First is the general contractor who organizes a project, hires other contractors to act as subcontractors, and is responsible for coordinating the activities of these subcontractors through the completion of the project. For example, the general contractor may be a home builder who engages the services of excavating contractors, carpenters, plumbers, electricians, and others to build a single home for a client. This operation is usually referred to as a "turnkey" because the general contractor bundles the services of several subcontractors into a single contract with his or her client.

The second type of contractor is the independent contractor. These contractors work one-on-one with their clients and do not work under the direction of a general contractor. Many projects will have both types of contractors working in conjunction with each other. A client may hire a general contractor to build a new home and also hire, under separate contracts, a landscape contractor to plan and install the outdoor spaces, a driveway installer to lay asphalt, and an irrigation company to install an automatic sprinkler system.

This book will focus on those contractors, both general and independent, who provide the services and material required to develop homes, office buildings, subdivisions, and similar projects. If you have the desire to become what we'll call a "property development" contractor, then this book is for you. We'll help you determine if you are the right type of person for such an undertaking. Then, we'll discuss the nitty-gritty of getting started. A lot of time will be spent on how to profitably price your product and service. Troubleshooting problem employees and clients will be another important topic. Finally, we'll tell you why it's important to PANIC in order to be successful.

The Players

Developing a property can be a very complex and time-consuming undertaking. A wide range of experts are needed for a successful property development project. In general, there are two types of contractors involved with the development process: those who generally work on the inside of a building and those who work on the exterior of the building or on the landscape. Following is a list of contractors found working at property development projects. The list is not inclusive; there are additional contractors who have a special niche in the industry. Some contractors specialize in maintenance and repair, while others work with new construction; many do both.

Inside contractors include:

- ▶ Architects
- ▶ Engineers
- ▶ Interior designers
- ▶ Carpenters
- ▶ Plumbers
- ▶ Electricians
- ▶ Cabinetmakers
- ▶ Drywall contractors
- ▶ Flooring and tiling contractors
- ▶ Heating and air-conditioning specialists
- ▶ Insulation contractors
- ▶ Painters and paperhangers
- ▶ Security systems specialists
- ▶ Masons

warning

The feds are watching you closely. If you are hiring subcontractors it is your responsibility to pay them in full at the agreed-upon rate. The rates of subcontractors should be factored into the pay applications so that when the client pays you, the money for your subcontracts will be included. Contractors have landed in jail for failing to pay subcontractors in full. Don't cut corners, or you can ruin your reputation and end up in hot water.

Outside contractors include:

- ▶ Landscape architects
- ▶ Engineers
- ▶ Grading and excavating companies
- ▶ Asphalt companies
- ▶ Lighting experts
- ▶ Irrigation specialists
- ▶ Landscape contractors
- ▶ Surveyors
- ▶ Deck and patio builders
- ▶ Painters
- ▶ Swimming pool builders
- ▶ Waterproofers

The United States Department of Labor Occupational Safety and Health Administration (OSHA) also adds a number of specialty trade contractors including those that work on mobile homes, those involved with bridge painting, as well as special trade contractors primarily engaged in activities that are clearly linked to specialization in the area of heavy construction, such as grading for highways and airport runways; guardrail construction; installation of highway signs; underwater rock removal; and asphalt and concrete construction of roads, highways, streets, and public sidewalks. You'll also find specialists in masonry, stonework, tile setting, plastering, and so forth. The point is, contract specialists can be found in almost any possible area of expertise.

Contractors most often, except on very small jobs, will work in teams. For example, a landscape architect will be responsible for the design of the exterior of the property, and an architect will design the building itself. Each may be responsible for ensuring that her designs are properly built. Each may hire other contractors to complete the work. These subcontractors usually work for the architect/landscape architect and not for the owner of the property. They will schedule their work with the architect/landscape architect who, in turn, will coordinate the activities of all the subcontractors.

Another type of contractor is the design/build firm. This type of contracting company has trained architects and/or designers who provide plans for the development, assist the owners with obtaining the required permits for construction, and provide their own work force to complete the actual construction. In some cases, subcontractors may be used for services that the design/build company does not provide. These are usually very skilled services such as cabinetmaking, or work that requires expensive equipment such as bulldozers and backhoes.

Of course, a property owner can act as his own general contractor. However, in order to be successful, the owner must have the time to coordinate all the activities. Typically, he should be on-site daily to be sure that materials are delivered on time and that subcontractors are performing their work according to the plans. It's also very important that the property owner authorizes all changes in the plans when necessary. (Imagine going on vacation for a week and returning to the project the following Monday morning and finding that your brand-new kitchen was painted metallic gold rather than the soft yellow you thought you had selected.) While creativity can be a plus, making sure everything you do is authorized, in writing, is essential in this industry. This is true whether or not the business or home owner is on the property.

There is nothing worse during the course of a project than having to undo work that has already been done. Imagine you are the general contractor, and the driveway contractor has just completed his work: excavating and grading, installation of a 12-inch gravel base, and then laying three inches of asphalt. Then, the next day your plumber shows up with a huge backhoe and informs you that he must dig a trench eight-feet deep right through your new driveway so that he can install the septic system.

These are nightmare scenarios that have actually happened. Proper time management and knowledge of all facets of the work are vitally important to a successful project. Contractors of all types must know not only their own areas of expertise but also the sequence of the project and be able to communicate with, and understand the basic work of, the other contractors working on the project.

Economic Importance

The contracting industry is vital to the economy of the United States. During good economic times, contractors are often the engine that keeps a local economy vibrant. In fact, according to the Engineering News-Record (at www.enr.com), the top 400 contracting companies in the United States generated over $330 billion in revenue in 2014. Whenever you drive past a new subdivision, take a look at the number of different types of trucks and

stat fact

According to industry sources, 90 percent of businesses in the U.S. construction industry employ fewer than 20 workers. Small construction businesses are a critical part of a vital economic sector and the U.S. economy as a whole.

vans that enter the development each morning; note the different types of equipment being used by these workers. And think about the families that these workers are supporting. Their work helps support industries like department and appliance stores, grocery stores, and restaurants. During times of economic struggle, the most creative of these companies remain busy and viable with remodeling projects as well as providing maintenance and repair services. However when building and development slow down, the entire economy suffers as many employers lay off portions of their staff.

Recent data (according to www.investopedia.com) indicates that in spite of the major recession of 2008–2009, entrepreneurship in the United States is alive and well, and the construction and contracting industries are growing. In fact, half of the top ten fastest-growing industries in the United States, as of 2015, are tied to the construction industry. Not only have construction revenues grown but unemployment has dropped considerably in the industry.

While the contracting industry is not for the faint of heart, for those who have the resources, the talent, and the desire to become a contractor, the rewards can be substantial. Not only financial rewards but also quality of life issues are enhanced by owning your own successful contracting business.

So grab your hard hat, and jump right in to learn what it takes to become a successful and profitable contractor.

aha!

If you are currently working for a contractor and plan to open your own business, don't assume that your customers will automatically move their business to your new company. Most customers are more loyal to a business than to an individual employee. You may, however, serve a niche market and can handle business opportunities in an area of expertise in conjunction with your former contractor and/or other established contractors.

Wrap-Up

▶ The contracting industry is very large and diverse.

▶ Contractors are important and valuable contributors to local and regional economies.

▶ Profitable and rewarding opportunities abound for creative and talented entrepreneurs.

Why Become a Contractor?

Becoming a contractor is a unique endeavor because contractors work out among their fellow citizens, unlike most retail or professional businesses who draw customers to their establishments. Contractors, on the other hand, spend most of their time away from their office or their home base. Typically they are working in apartment buildings, client's offices, or on the property of real estate owners.

Contractors Are Important to Their Communities

Contractors do much more than develop property. In many ways they improve their clients' and communities' quality of life . For many clients, their homes are their castles, their property, their domains. They spend countless hours in and around their homes and feel it's important to be comfortable with their surroundings. Of course they all have their own individual likes and dislikes. While one may require a quiet but colorful garden for introspective thought, another may need a high-tech "great room" for entertaining friends and family. For many businesses, image is an important factor in their success. Perhaps a large fountain with multicolored lights is what they need, or a comfortable meeting room with the latest in high-tech communications devices. Most municipalities have specific requirements and standards for the design of subdivisions, park land, and urban spaces. Creative contractors meet the varying needs of all these groups, completing their work in ways that will improve the health and welfare of the community.

Contractors also improve and ensure the safety of their clients. Proper design and construction of the spaces that people use for living, working, and recreation ensure a safe environment for these activities. Contractors must be knowledgeable about local building codes as well as industry-accepted methods of installation. Construction contractors improve the safety of the community by:

► Providing safe working conditions for their employees
► Requiring employees to use safety equipment such as eye/ear protection and hard hats
► Ensuring that buildings are fire safe
► Using construction materials that ensure the structural integrity of a building
► Designing proper surface grading to provide acceptable drainage of rainwater
► Installing handicap ramps and railings to meet building codes
► Installing septic systems for environmental safety
► Utilizing sight safety triangles at roadway and driveway intersections for safe driving conditions

Owning and managing your own business can be very rewarding—both mentally and financially. However, do not think that it is always a bed of roses. Operating your own business is much like a rose garden. The vibrant colors of the garden provide beauty and joy to passersby, but for those who get too close and do not pay attention to what they are doing, the sharp thorns can cause pain and discomfort. As you will learn later in the book, paying close attention to the details of your daily work will keep you from being stuck by the thorny issues that surround most businesses.

Do You Have What It Takes?–Part I

Contractors come in all sizes, shapes, and temperaments. But the one trait they all seem to have in common is a burning desire to start and operate their own business. If you have this burning desire to become your own boss, to work independently, to make all the important decisions required to run a successful business and you are willing to assume full responsibility for your decisions, you pass the first test on starting your own business. You also have to be willing to spend long hours and make many personal sacrifices to achieve success. There will be times when your family life will need to make sacrifices because of the demands of your business. Do you have a good partner or spouse who understands and accepts these demands? Starting a business is difficult and stressful. It's very important to have a supportive family to get through the tough times when running your own business. Finally, you need to have enough self-confidence to stand by your decisions as well as enough self-discipline to persevere and build your new business.

One of the intangible and hard-to-define qualities found in the most effective business owners is the ability to stand back and look at the big picture. Much like the race car drivers of the past, successful business owners must be able to understand and recognize the multitude of situations that affect the daily activities of their business. The race car driver, for obvious reasons, is concerned with speed. However, pure speed is not the only factor in winning the race. While driving as fast as he can, the driver must be aware of tire pressure, engine temperature, and the front end of the car that controls steering, among many other things, such as the positions of the other cars on the track. These factors influence both the speed and the sustainability of the car. Low tire pressure will make the car more difficult to steer, which will affect speed; high engine temperature will effect engine performance and also reduce speed.

tip

You can find accredited colleges in architecture, landscape architecture, and engineering. Go to the National Architectural Accrediting Board at www.naab.org. The American Society of Landscape Architects at https://asla.org/schools.aspx or the American Society of Engineering Education at www.asee.org.

The driver must be able to look at the big picture and understand how the smallest of details interact and influence the final result of the race. The best drivers are also able to look at an anomaly and realize that it may not affect the performance of their car. Today, drivers, much like modern business owners, are assisted by computer technology and a team that helps to interpret the data. But this help does not reduce the importance of understanding how the numerous bits and pieces of a business react and influence each other—and when to ignore what seems to be a problem when it is of little or no significance to the operation of the business. Today's technology provides various tools for race car drivers and for contractors. The key is knowing how to utilize such tools to your advantage and when to use them.

Do You Have the Proper Background?

Individual skills are extremely important to succeeding in the contracting industry. Some are natural, and many can be learned. The ability to use and improve both natural and learned skills is an important factor in developing a successful business. Either way, it is important to develop your skills to the highest possible level.

Those of you who have a desire to enter the design field, such as architecture or landscape architecture, must have artistic and creative instincts. The ability to think abstractly and visualize outcomes is extremely important. Creative solutions to development challenges separate the outstanding firm from the average one. Most industry associations have annual awards competitions where companies or individuals have the opportunity to present their best projects, their best ideas, to their peers. The most creative of these projects stand out and set the standards of excellence for their respective industries.

However, natural skill and ability is not enough.

Consider professional athletes. From 1997 through 2008 Tiger Woods won 14 of the 48 major golf tournaments. But Tiger did not get to the top merely by using the talents he was born with. His father worked tirelessly with young Tiger to hone his skills; he perfected his swing and trained his mind to withstand the rigors of intense competition. Even after winning many major golf tournaments, Tiger kept working with his coaches to improve his swing so that he could continue to stay ahead of the competition. Other athletes like Michael Jordan would arrive an hour early before pre-game warm-ups to take shot after shot. This wasn't during his early years learning the game but during his amazing NBA career. The best of the best don't stop once they've made it to the top; they continue working hard to stay there, always pushing themselves. At any level, you can always work on enhancing your current skills while learning new ones.

Formal Education

Architects, landscape architects, engineers, and others in the professional field typically earn undergraduate or graduate degrees in their field. Four years of college are required for an undergraduate degree and an additional two years for a master's degree. Many colleges will allow students to earn a master's degree even if their undergraduate degree is in a field unrelated to architecture, landscape architecture, or engineering.

tip

The website www. collegeboard.org has an extensive search engine for finding colleges of all types throughout the United States.

There are excellent opportunities for those who do not wish, or are unable, to attend a full four-year college program. Technical schools, usually offering two-year degree programs, are a great place to learn a new trade or to improve a skill you presently have. These programs do not require the rigorous high school curriculum and pre-admission testing needed to be accepted at four-year colleges. Technical schools offer degrees in the construction trades such as plumbing, carpentry, and landscaping. They also offer programs in business management, marketing, and real estate for those who intend on someday starting their own business in the property development industry. Currently nearly 2,000 technical schools in the United States offer associate degree programs in the construction trades and/or horticulture/landscaping.

On-the-Job Training (OJT)

Those of you who have been in the military likely understand the term "OJT." After surviving eight weeks of torturous basic training, you were given an MOS (military occupational specialty) and assigned to a post. If, for example, the Army decided that it needed a clerk-typist, you might be assigned to a company headquarters office to learn typing and filing. No experience needed; just show up for work, and your superior would show you what to do. Over the following weeks and months, you'd learn your job while doing it. Little, if any, formal education was provided. If you learned the job quickly, you'd be promoted from private to specialist, and hopefully to sergeant. Each promotion would bring more responsibility and higher wages.

In the construction business OJT is a common way for employees to learn the trade. New, inexperienced employees are assigned to a work crew led by an experienced foreman or crew leader. It's the job of the foreman to complete each job or project according to the specifications established for the project and to finish it at or under budget. Her job is also to train new employees on how to do their particular tasks. As in the military, new employees are given simple tasks at first and then move on to more complex and skilled work as they master each task. Repetition and familiarity with the necessary tools will help facilitate OJT.

An important part of OJT is making mistakes! All employees (as well as bosses and business owners) will make mistakes at some time during their career, and new employees typically make more mistakes than more experienced ones. The key to mistakes is the ability to learn from them. As a boss or business owner, you should make it a point to encourage employees to understand what they did wrong and move forward. Those who do learn from mistakes and errors eventually become much better and more productive employees. And, most important for those who intend on starting their own contracting business, understanding and learning from your past mistakes will make you a better teacher of new employees; the result will be that your business is more productive, successful, and profitable.

Lloyd Price

Your first reaction is probably "Who?" Well, back in the early days of rock 'n' roll music, before the Beatles became famous, an up-and-coming singer from New Orleans named Lloyd Price released a hit record called "(You've Got) Personality."

Now don't get us wrong, were not saying that business owners who have a strong personality will instantly become successful. However, personality is part of what can set you apart from your competition. People do business with other people, especially those with whom they like spending time. Why do people pay more at specialty shops when most items can be found for less money in big-box stores or on the internet? They have developed a rapport with the store owner, manager, or even someone working in sales. Consider the spokesmen and women for businesses; they speak on behalf of the company because they have personalities to which others gravitate. This doesn't mean you have to be boisterous or even outgoing. All it means is that you need to be personable, polite, attentive, respectful, and communicate well with others, which also means being a very good listener. Being personable is just one of several character traits that will help you as a business owner; here are a few others.

Discipline and Determination

Think about great professional golfers in both the PGA and LPGA. They all combine their natural athletic ability with discipline and determination. They are disciplined in the way they practice and in the way they approach each shot. Week in and week out, they practice and set up each shot in precisely the same way. They are also determined enough to keep their minds on the game and their goal (of winning) always in sight. They have incredible ability to focus on the task at hand; the last shot they made, good or bad, is a distant memory and has absolutely no effect on their next shot. They also persevere through good times and bad. Consider golfer Phil Mickelson, who won the Masters Tournament in 2004 after laboring on the PGA tour for 12 years. Likewise, you need to have the determination to make a project fit the needs of the client(s) and the discipline to stay on task no matter what goes wrong along the way (and something always goes wrong). Very few projects go smoothly form start to finish, so you must stay the course and be determined that it WILL work out well in the end.

Self-Confidence

Self-confidence is critical. Business ownership is often a lonely life. President Harry Truman had a sign on his desk that read, "The Buck Stops Here," indicating that he was responsible for decision making. He could not pass crucial decisions on to someone else. Similarly, in order to start and run a successful contracting business, the owner must be willing to make key decisions, often alone. However, one of the biggest decisions that most business owners make is deciding when they need to call in someone else. Self-confidence should not be confused with stubbornness. We all have our knowledge and skill sets, but we also have to know what we don't know and reach out for help when necessary. Heads of Fortune 500 companies and leaders of industries do not get to those positions by trying to do it all alone; they reach out to experts in all kinds of fields for help. That's real self-confidence.

Good Health

Operating a contracting business is both physically and mentally stressful. Early mornings, followed by long days, and six-day weeks are very common throughout the contracting industry. Contractors must be in excellent health, both physically and mentally, in order to achieve success. Exercise and a good, healthy diet is advised.

Excellent Time Management Skills

A well-organized manager earns the respect not only of fellow employees but also of clients. Every day an owner is bombarded with requests, and often these are really demands on his or her time. Foremen ask for direction about a current project; an assistant requests clarification of information needed to complete a job estimate; a client calls asking why some service was not done properly; a supplier calls to reschedule a delivery; and a magazine salesperson calls needing information for the current advertisement, which has a deadline of today. All this, and the owner has an important meeting with a prospective client in one hour. Oh yes, and don't forget to sign today's payroll checks. Most contracting businesses are like a busy beehive, especially in the morning. An owner must be able to prioritize his tasks, adjust the daily schedule to solve true emergencies, and keep the operation moving forward as smoothly as possible. Of particular importance in time management is organizing the work crews on a daily basis so that time is not wasted and clients are not kept waiting. Efficient foremen know exactly where they are going, what type of work they will do, and what tools they need to complete the job. If an owner is too busy with other tasks, money is lost while employees are getting paid to sit and wait for instructions.

Time management is important not only on a daily basis but also on a long-term basis. As the backlog of work increases, owners must be able to accurately project how long each project will take so that they can accurately schedule future projects. One of the worst things a contracting company can do is promise a client "we'll be there next week" and then, for no reason apparent to the client, show up in three weeks. A company may use a chart like the one in the sample work schedule (Figure 2–1) or any of numerous time management programs, many of which are mobile, such as the mJobTime Mobility Suite (at www.mjobtime.com), which helps you track projects and keep everyone updated with modules for the labor manager, GPS manager, equipment manager, daily field manager, budgets manager and documents manager. Procore Management Software (at www.procore.com) also has several products designed for general contractors, engineering firms, and construction management firms to handle time management and project coordination. ExakTime (at www.exaktime.com) is another of several companies with software, and mobile apps, to help you with time tracking. Look for time management tools online. Ironically, they can save you time and help you communicate what needs to be addressed sooner than later to your subcontractors and/or employees.

In the "Sample Work Schedule" shown in Figure 2–1, page 15, if another client, Mr. Allen, prefers to work with Charlie, the owner knows that he cannot promise to start the Allen project until early June. Similarly, if Jane is extremely talented in a particular task, the owner knows he cannot send her out to complete this type of work until late May.

Time management encompasses much more then merely organizing a daily calendar. It is crucial to the success of a contracting business.

Do You Have What It Takes?–Part II

Beyond character traits are a host of abilities that contractors must have in order to succeed. The best and most successful contractors have a good balance of technical

Work Schedule

Foreman	May 1	May 8	May 15	May 22
Charlie	Johnson	Jones O'Brien	Smith	Mueller
Jane	Wilson Hellman	Carson	Carson	(open)
Andy	Murphy	McCarthy	(open)	(open)

FIGURE 2–1: **Sample Work Schedule**
A tracking chart like this will help you manage employees, available subcontractors, and jobs.

skills and business management expertise. As you learned earlier, many contractors are blessed with the natural skills to do their jobs. Most are craftsmen and women who pay careful attention to detail, avoid sloppy work, and finish their work with confidence and pride. They are able to step back from a completed project and say to themselves and their co-workers, "Job well done!" They are confident that their clients will say the same thing.

Continuing Education

As skilled as they may be, many contractors like to keep up to date with the latest advances in their field by taking advantage of opportunities for continuing education. Along with returning to school for a degree as mentioned earlier, there are many avenues available for learning about new products and techniques.

► Seminars presented by suppliers of the materials a contractor purchases.

► How-to seminars given by home improvement stores like Home Depot and Lowe's.

► Conferences and classes offered or sponsored by industry associations.

► College courses (not as part of a degree program) on campus and/or online are available on anything from general contracting to general

save

Use the internet and do a Google search for "contractor magazines," and find opportunities to receive free magazine subscriptions that focus on your specialty.

construction management to pipefitting and sprinkler fitting. Such courses can be found at http://Learn.org or http://Study.com, which provides a similar listing of courses. You can also check local college course listings in your area.

▶ Industry-specific magazines, newspapers, blogs, or websites.

▶ The government-sponsored Small Business Administration (www.sba.gov) also offers education and help to all small businesses.

Tools

Contractors don't like to admit it, but many lay people, including their clients, are able to do similar work. Perhaps not quite as well and certainly not as fast, but they can do many tasks that contractors are experts at. The DIY (do-it-yourself) retail market is huge; the combined revenues of Home Depot and Lowe's are over $120 billion, representing over 70 percent of the industry; several cable television stations, such as HGTV, also specialize in home improvement and remodeling. And if you do a Google search on how to do a certain type of project, chances are you'll find it.

However, beyond their natural skills and personalities, contractors possess two things that most of the public does not have. First, they have the time to do the work. Most homeowners and amateurs can only work nights and weekends; their regular jobs prevent them from working full time on their projects. Most homeowners do not want to live in their homes for extended periods without running water or with a hole in the roof, or go through the entire winter without a driveway. Contractors have the ability to complete a project quickly and with minimal disruption to their client's household.

Second, contractors have the right tools to do the job. While the equipment rental business is fairly large, many homeowners are uncomfortable using expensive tools. Some tools and equipment are not available for rent due to liability issues; other equipment, such as a dump truck, usually is not available on a short-term basis. Often, when a homeowner rents a particular tool, he botches the job because he does not have enough experience to use it properly.

Having the right tools is one of the keys to success in the contracting industry. A landscape contractor reported to us that when he first started he used a handheld sod remover when preparing plant beds; on one of his first jobs, he and a worker spent the better part of two days removing sod by hand. The result was not only sore arms and tendonitis in his wrists but a lower profit due to the time it took to do the task. The next week he purchased a gas-powered sod cutter for several thousand dollars, a very large expense for the young company. But the time savings he achieved by using newer and better technology allowed him to pay for the sod cutter in a single season. Instead of spending two days removing sod, he was able to complete the same work in a few hours, with less manpower as well. In fact, his sales and profits actually increased because he was able to move on to the next job much more quickly.

Learn the Lingo

Contactors often work together to finish projects. Their working relationship may not be formal as they might merely be working on a project at the same time. However, many contractor jobs overlap. Contractors have to understand what the others are doing so that they do not "step on each other's toes." All of them should be able to read and understand blueprints of the building and the landscaping so that the materials they are installing do not interfere or conflict with what the other contractor is doing. For example, the irrigation contractor must be able to read the landscape plan and the grading plan in order to efficiently design the sprinkler system; the low-voltage outdoor lighting specialist must understand the electrical plans in order to design a lighting plan that reduces voltage drop and does not conflict with the full-voltage lights specified for the home.

A development project comes together more successfully when all the participants understand each other's responsibilities and what the scope of their work includes. While they do not necessarily need to know how to do the work of the other contractors, they must understand the concepts and terminology used by them.

Money Issues

President Thomas Jefferson once wrote, "Never spend your money before you have it." This little truism has wide implications for the contracting industry because of the seasonal and cyclical nature of the business. In Chapter 6 we discuss how to establish a budget and the importance of cash flow. But first there are two important issues relating to money that everyone contemplating starting up his or her own business should understand.

A Nest Egg

Conventional wisdom states that a new business owner should have savings in the bank to cover at least six months of personal expenses. Every potential business owner must take the time to learn how much money he or she has spent over the past 12 months and estimate total expenses for the next six months. The attitude should be "since I will be working without a guaranteed income stream, how will I survive for at least the next six months?" Use your checkbook, bank statement, or credit/debit card statements to compile a list of all your projected expenses—mortgage, taxes, utilities, insurance, food, and recreation. If your spouse has a secure job, his or her take-home pay can be used to reduce the amount of savings you need. If you do not have the ready cash to survive at least six months, you would be wise to postpone starting your business until you have the necessary funds.

These savings should be kept separately from your stock and bonds portfolio and invested in a conservative, high-yield money market account that offers free checking and has few, if any, fees. A couple of sources for information are www.bankrate.com and the online *Money* magazine at http://time.com/money. Many other financial magazines also include up-to-date interest rate information on a weekly basis. The goal, however, is safety and low-risk security for yourself and your family.

Startup Funds

Beyond providing a nest egg for personal living, any new business also needs enough capital to survive six months to one year of business. Because it usually takes some time for a new enterprise to attract enough business to ensure a secure cash flow, having enough ready cash is critical. Operating expenses include salaries, wages, rent, utilities, supplies, advertising, and perhaps bank and interest payments. Sources of these funds are usually loans from banks or individuals and accumulated personal savings or loans against your life insurance policy if you have one. You do not want to put your home at risk with a home equity loan nor do you want to run up high-interest credit card debt or dip into money in your retirement portfolio, which you'll need for your future.

A Good Credit Rating

The financial demands on a new contracting company can be enormous. Not only do employees expect to receive their wages every week or two, suppliers expect to be paid every month, possibly even within ten days. Clients, on the other hand, often do not see an urgency to pay immediately upon completion of the work. Some clients seem to think that contractors are banks and that they can pay off their invoice over several months. This situation should be avoided by requesting a down payment from a client before the work begins. However, a key ingredient to success is earning a good credit rating so that your suppliers will send you a bill once a month for the items you purchased. A good credit rating will also allow you to purchase vehicles and equipment and borrow the funds from your bank.

The problem with buying materials on credit is the ability to pay in a timely manner without incurring late and/or finance charges. While credit is a good way to maintain current cash flow, it is not a substitute for having available funding. A rule of thumb is to use debt by intention and not by default. In other words, have the money available and do not buy on credit (or hire people on credit) with hopes that the money will show up.

Chapter 6 delves into the subject of managing your cash flow in much more detail. Remember, a good credit rating will allow you to establish charge accounts at your suppliers, but only by paying the suppliers according to their requirements will you maintain your good credit rating.

There are three companies in the United States that maintain credit information on individuals: Equifax, Experian, and TransUnion LLC. Contact information on these companies may be found in the Appendix. It is a good idea to check your credit rating from time to time to ensure that there are no errors in the report.

Management Expertise

An important piece of the puzzle needed to answer the question "Do you have what it takes?" is the ability to manage the enterprise. You have seen that contractors must be able to manage their own time, be disciplined, and be self-reliant. However, they must also be able to manage the activities and turmoil that usually surround them on a daily basis. A workplace is a dynamic community of people with varying backgrounds. While it is true that a company is much like a family, it is also an individual business. Often business decisions conflict with personal feelings; good managers must be able to separate emotion from hard reality.

Managing People

Managing people is a true art. People have their own personalities that are sometimes in conflict with one another. However, because they work for the same organization, they must be able to work together for a common goal. As a contractor-owner it is up to you to promote a work environment in which people focus at the task at hand and keep their personal opinions on outside matters, especially politics and religion, to themselves.

You have heard about the sports team whose talent is not highly regarded; however, its coach has the ability to push each player and enable them to perform at a level above their natural talents. He's able to generate positive chemistry on the team, with the result that the individual team members play their best and the team wins the championship.

For a more specific example, let's assume that Joe is a long-term employee who has much in common with the boss: Both attended college in the same city, love to play

tip

Get to know your banker! It is not enough just to swing by the bank and make deposits; you should get to know a personal banker at the branch where you do your banking. Over time, she will understand your business and your financial needs. She'll be in a good position to advise you about interest rates, borrowing, and how to best manage your cash.

golf, and have sons enrolled in the same school; they often see each other at functions unrelated to their jobs. However, for personal family reasons, Joe's production, attitude, and attendance have become a problem. The boss has several discussions with Joe who becomes more defensive and angry with each meeting. Joe's behavior finally begins to negatively affect several of the office staff. The result is that company sales decline, the atmosphere in the office is dark and dismal, productivity suffers, and clients become upset with their service. Ultimately the boss will have to make the difficult decision as to whether or not to fire Joe. He will have to put personal feelings aside, take a look at the big picture, and make the ultimate decision about Joe's fate.

aha!

For some training on leadership and how to hone such skills there are many great books to read and even courses to take, such as those offered online by Dale Carnegie Training at www.dalecarnegie.com/online-training. You might also read his classic book, *How to Win Friends and Influence People.*

Communication Management

Successful business owners must have excellent communication skills. Time, money, and reputation can be lost by owners who do not communicate clearly with both employees and clients. Many clients have preconceived ideas about what a contractor should do; oftentimes they do not read contracts and proposals carefully enough to really understand what they are getting. Usually, they do not understand blueprints; sometimes, they have a vision from a photograph in a home improvement magazine. It's critical that a contractor-owner have the ability to clearly explain the services he offers and exactly what he proposes to do for the client. In the case of landscaping, it's important that the client understand that it takes time for a landscape to mature; unlike a new kitchen or bathroom, the final product is not realized immediately upon completion of the work.

Owners must also be able to accurately communicate with employees. Because projects are often changed and adjusted midstream, good communication between the owner and the foreman is needed for the project to proceed accurately and on time. In addition, two-dimensional drawings are sometimes difficult to translate into the three-dimensional world. The contractor must not only communicate what must be done with accurate and legible drawings but also be able to explain verbally what the drawings mean.

Modern communication is most often conducted through cell phones (primarily iPhones or Android smartphones) and emails as well as texts. While this is fine for setting up meetings and having initial conversations, it does not replace in-person, on-site communications, which are imperative to real-world projects. In-person and on-site meetings are essential throughout the process, especially in the early stages or when changes need to be discussed and made.

The most important communication between clients and contractors are the specifics of each project, and they must be confirmed, reconfirmed, and signed off on. Communication must therefore be very clear with each and everyone working on the project. Emails and texts must be simple and to the point, and there needs to be a response confirming that such an email or text was received and acknowledged. You also want a paper trail, and/or electronic trail, on all important communications, especially when changes are requested and agreed upon.

Fortunately, smartphones allow for communication from anyplace and the ability to look at specs and other data at both ends of the conversation, as well as photos and diagrams. Make sure that all key personnel have the latest in mobile tools to make communication that much easier.

Organization Management

How many times have you heard someone say, "The left hand doesn't know what the right hand is doing." As business owners, you would much rather hear, "It went off like clockwork." Contractors are often away from the office much of the day, and unless they have a very small family business, they do not really know what happens at the office. Employees are very aware of a disorganized boss who is out-of-touch with the day-to-day operations of the office and runs from one task to another in a seemingly haphazard way. Most owners are not aware of the office gossip and whispers that make the rounds; they probably would be appalled at what they would hear. Unfortunately, an owner's own chaotic style often filters down to the office staff. However, if an owner implements a good organizational chart, with the assistance of employees who perform the work, each employee will know his own responsibilities and, as important, the responsibilities of every other employee. In this way the company will operate more efficiently, profitably, and mistake-free. Chapter 9 goes into more detail about organizational charts.

Send in the Delegation

A key to organizational success is the ability of an entrepreneur to delegate responsibilities to other employees. Very few business owners have the ability to perform all the tasks required to operate their business. They are likely to be experts at some things, very good at others, and nearly hopeless at others. Because most entrepreneurs have loads of confidence in their abilities, it is hard for many to admit to themselves, "I'm not very good in this area, I need help, and this is how I intend to achieve it."

Delegating authority to others can be a difficult task not only because it may be hard to find the right person to handle the tasks but also because it is hard for an entrepreneur to give up some of the control of his business. The process of delegating involves four steps:

stat fact

According to National Association of Home Builders, homeowners spent about $150 billion on home improvements and repairs in 2013. That was 16 percent less than in 2011 ($178 billion).

1. Finding good people who are trustworthy and have the expertise to be successful in the area concerned.
2. Hiring the person and incorporating him into your company.
3. Clearly communicating what is expected of them and how to find answers, or know who to contact, if there is a problem.
4. Giving someone else the ball, and allowing that person to run with it.

The best entrepreneurs routinely monitor the activities of these employees but do not constantly look over their shoulders, micromanage their activities, or reverse their decisions without very good cause.

While the ability to delegate is important, over-delegating can become a problem. The owner may become too far removed from the daily activities of the business. The art of delegating is also the art of team building; owners must understand how all the pieces of the business fit together to form the whole. The risk in over-delegating is that decision making becomes too decentralized, communication breaks down, and the business becomes inefficient.

Wrap-Up

- ► Contractors enhance the safety of individuals as well as the community at large.
- ► Contractor-owners have the burning desire to operate their own business and have the knowledge and experience, either through formal education or on-the-job training, to be successful.
- ► As business owners, contractors must be disciplined and determined, self-reliant, in good health, and practice excellent time management.
- ► Contractors have the advantage over the general public because they keep up with the latest advances in their particular field, have the best tools to do the job, and understand the common terminology used in the various disciplines of the property development industry.

▶ Contractors can be successful if their finances are in good order, they have the ability to manage people, can communicate effectively with employees and clients, and they know how to organize their employees and/or subcontractors for maximum efficiency.

▶ The ability to delegate responsibilities is critical to success.

The Business Plan

A business plan is a written document that summarizes how a business owner intends to organize the business and how it will run and earn a profit so that the business will succeed. It defines the strategy that will be used to establish, operate, and market the venture. The business plan has value because it forces the entrepreneur to engage in the planning process through which she will gain a better understanding of the industry, the business, and the various options available. It is also an essential selling point when looking to obtain loans from banks or individual investors.

Business plans come in many forms. Many are very detailed documents while others are more informal. A typical outline of a business plan follows.

Executive Summary

The executive summary must be impressive because it is the first thing people read in your plan, and we all know the power of a strong first impression. This is where you want to wow people. It is like the coming attraction, or trailer, at the movie theater. You want it to highlight the business idea and make readers want to find out more. While it is at the beginning of the business plan, it is often written last after all of the pieces of the plan have been determined.

Features and Advantages of Your Products or Services

At this point you need to describe what it is you do and how you do it. As a service business, you need to lay out what services you provide and what expertise your business brings to the table. Also, answer the question: What makes your services different from those of other, similar, businesses?

The Market/Industry

Illustrate, briefly, the market your business will be a part of. Be specific and show how and why this is a growing market. Also demonstrate how you fit into this market. It's hard to prove you belong in an oversaturated market, so do your homework to make sure there is room for you to compete in your city or town. Since a contracting business is dependent on a location, define the industry in the local market.

If need be, find a niche to fill in an otherwise crowded market and explain why you are invaluable. Also make sure you explain your demographic market and discuss your competition, not from a negative approach, but simply by explaining your competitive edge over other similar businesses.

Marketing

Your marketing plan is all about knowing your target audience and explaining how you are going to reach out to them. Before including this in your business plan, do your homework and figure out where potential customers look for such services. For example, if you remodel kitchens and bathrooms, you will market yourself on websites and in magazines that homeowners or builders look at. However, before you can start reaching out to potential customers, you also need to define what services you are selling, at what price(s) ,and in what location(s). Also discuss your pricing strategy (are you competing with low prices or perhaps providing specialized services to discerning customers who are willing to pay). To simplify, you can use the four Ps of marketing: product, price, place, and promotion.

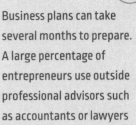

stat fact

Business plans can take several months to prepare. A large percentage of entrepreneurs use outside professional advisors such as accountants or lawyers for help; many also attend business plan seminars.

The census website at http://census.gov is a great place to start searching for demographic data. You can also learn a lot about marketing research by going to the Marketing Research Association at www.marketingresearch.org.

Management and Key Personnel

It's important when doing a business plan to feature yourself first. After all, you are the person, the entrepreneur, behind the business venture, and it is you who will have to put your neck on the line, answer the hard questions, and take the criticism—as well as the praise and acclaim, should there be some.

Many people invest largely because they believe in the owner and the management team. Provide key information on each person on the team. If you are a one-person operation, explain how you can handle the jobs and from where you will hire subcontractors. Explain your criteria for such hires and compensation. You should also include outside advisors, such as lawyers, accountants, or financial consultants, and describe their backgrounds and input into your business. If you have a management team, or advisory team, briefly describe the background of each member and what makes that person important to your business.

Operations or Production

An Operations or Production section is all about how you do what you do. This can cover a lot of ground in a short section where you include a description of your services; sourcing raw materials, hiring labor, acquiring facilities and equipment; and how you complete and get paid for a project. Also include the overall costs of equipment such as tools, a truck (or several), and both office and mobile communications tools. Then discuss what you will do both on- and off-site and your access to the necessary materials you will need to complete a project. Where will you buy them and store them?

The basic rule for your operations section is to cover all the major areas including labor, materials, facilities, equipment, processes, and payment to illustrate the details that are critical to your business operation.

Finance

Your goal in this section is to explain how your business will work from a financial perspective. You want to show the projections of expenses and sales over one, three, and even five years. Be conservative in your estimates, and always have the math ready to back them up. Make sure you include existing liabilities coming into the business. You can typically gather information and use Excel or another financial software program to make the spreadsheets you'll need to support your written overview of your future financial picture. Business plan software is also readily available with the necessary spreadsheets.

The most important financial statement you will need is an income statement (also known as a profit and loss statement (P&L) or an earnings statement. Income statements answer the questions, "Am I making or losing money?" and "How?" A cash-flow statement can show how you will stay liquid, which is vital to any business, and a break-even analysis will show that you have a good idea of what you need to reach before you can come out with a profit. You should also let it be known how much money you are putting into the business since investors will always take a project more seriously if they know you have invested in the undertaking.

Risk Planning

It's important for you and for your investors to know that you are accounting for risks, which can include anything from unfavorable industry-wide growth trends, to low sales to lack of skilled labor to a major competitor undercutting your process to a recession.

aha!

Mini business plans of five to ten pages have become the popular concise models that may stand on their own for smaller businesses. It's to your advantage to run long when creating your initial plan (15 to 20 pages) and then narrow it down for presentation purposes.

Many such presentations are made with PowerPoint decks, using 10 to 12 slides to tell your story. This is a great starting point, but you should have at least a more detailed mini-plan available, especially if you are seeking lots of money.

Whether you are using a version of Microsoft Word or one of the popular software programs to guide you along the way, you can go back to earlier versions and revise and rewrite as you go. Some people still enjoy printing out an early draft of their business plan and marking it up at the kitchen table, while others prefer reading everything on their computer and/or iPad, tablet, or iPhone.

Business plans can be 5 to 50 pages. More often than not, the smaller plans, or mini-plans, have become more fashionable in a world in which time is of the essence. Most plans today are sent electronically to potential investors, but you should be ready with hard copies if the situation presents itself. Also, you always want to double-check everything and proofread your work.

And finally, be ready to back up anything you have in your business plan and answer any questions a possible lender, investor, or potential vendor or partner may throw at you.

Business Plan Software

While you remain in the driver's seat, writing the plan and doing all the heavy thinking, business plan software can handle research, organization, calculations, and more.

save

There are many sources of information about how to prepare a business plan. One excellent source is the Small Business Administration (www.sba.gov), which provides assistance over the internet. Numerous books covering business plans such as *Write Your Business Plan* by Entrepreneur Media, Inc., can be found at Amazon (www.amazon.com), Barnes and Noble (www.barnesandnoble.com), and other online booksellers. You might also visit www.bplans.com, which is a very helpful website for anyone starting a business and writing a business plan.

Of course you don't have to use specific business plan software to write your plan. Microsoft Office or any similar software in which you can write each section of your plan can serve your purpose. You can even use Excel or other spreadsheet software to handle the financial pages.

However, should you want to the guidance of a software program, find one that meets your computer capabilities, has tech support readily available, and is highly rated. The difference between a $59 and $99 software program is typically the features.

Some of the most popular choices are: Business Plan Pro from Palo Alto Software at www.businessplanpro.com/; BizPlanBuilder® a cloud-based program from Jian software at www.businesspowertools.com/project/2015-a_bizplanbuilder-business-plan-software-template/;

and Ultimate Business Planner from Atlas Business Solutions at www.abs-usa.com/business-plan-software/overview.

Mission Statement

Every business has a purpose for its existence. A written mission statement, usually one to four sentences long, says what your company is, what you do, what you stand for, and why it's important. An example of a poorly written mission statement is: "We build fine homes." A much better example is: "We are dedicated to providing services and solutions that meet the dreams of our clients. Quality construction is delivered with friendliness, professionalism, individual pride, and company spirit." The best mission statements focus on satisfying customer needs rather than on the products that are sold. Certainly everyone wants to have a fine home, but it is more important for a client to know how he will get that fine home. The client will have positive feelings about hiring a company with a compelling and personal mission statement, and employees will understand the goals and objectives of the company they work for.

Financing Your Business

There are two ways to finance your new business: equity and debt. Equity financing involves raising money from investors who will often have an ownership stake in the new business.

Most small businesses start with the owner(s) putting some money into the project themselves. This will often encourage other investors, knowing that if the owner put his or her money into the business, then they are taking it seriously. Your investment should be money you have earmarked specifically for the business venture and NOT from your ongoing living expenses or your retirement savings. Other sources of funds often come from friends or relatives who have an interest in helping the new enterprise. Caution must be used when taking money from friends and relatives; personal relationships may be ruined if the business fails and these friends lose their investment. Business owners who raise capital in this manner must explain their business plan carefully and make it clear to potential investors that there are risks associated with their investment. It's also very important to stipulate whether such investors are going to be involved in the business or "silent" partners. Spell out everything, and put it on paper in advance.

Venture Capitalists

Venture capitalists (VCs) are another source of equity financing. These are wealthy individuals or companies who look for startups in which to invest their money. Generally, however, VCs prefer to invest in companies that have strong growth potential. VCs often like to get quite involved in the workings of the company and have less patience for businesses that project slow growth.

Angel Investors

Angels are individuals who invest their own money in new ventures of interest to them. Many angels are well-off professionals, such as doctors and lawyers or former business owners. Some are retired but have tremendous expertise to share in a specific field. Others are successful business owners who have made a bundle with their own entrepreneurial efforts and are now interested in letting their money work for them in someone else's venture. Typically they are less involved in the actual running of the business than VCs.

Angel investors used to be a difficult group to find. Not any longer. There are groups formed by angels and other organizations, such as Funding Post, that bring some angel investors together for you to meet. You can visit the Angel Capital Association (at www.angelcapitalassociation.org) or search on Google for "angel investing groups in" your area of the country.

Debt Financing

You can also seek out debt financing, which is achieved by borrowing money from a bank, credit union, or the U.S. Small Business Administration. These entities rely heavily on the business plan, financial forecasts, and the personal finances of the owners of the business. A new business is much more likely to obtain debt financing if the owners have committed a significant portion of the capital required for the business to get off the ground, have a good credit rating, and have a business plan that looks solid and sensible. They also like to know specifically what qualifications you have to run such a business.

One positive aspect of borrowing from banks or credit unions is that they don't want control—at least beyond the control exerted in the covenants of a loan document. And they don't want ownership. Bankers make loans, not investments, and as a general rule they don't want to wind up owning your company.

Loan covenants may require you to do all sorts of things, from setting a minimum amount of working capital you must maintain, to prohibiting you from

tip

When looking for sources of financing, go to Entrepreneur's website www.entrepreneur.com/bestbanks, and check out their up-to-date listing of best banks for entrepreneurs.

making certain purchases or signing leases without approval from the bank. For this reason, you want your accountant, financial advisor, and/or attorney to review your loan documents and spell out everything for you very carefully. Also review the many types of loans that are offered and determine which is best for your situation.

Credit Unions

According to the National Credit Union, there are more than 7,000 credit unions in the country with nearly 100 million members. Since credit unions are not-for-profit financial institutions, their focus is serving the financial needs of their members and not making a profit. As a result, once you have applied for membership and joined a credit union, it may be easier to get a lower interest rate with fewer fees than found at a bank when procuring a loan. However, like a bank, you will still need to prove your credit worthiness and that you can repay the loan, or have someone co-sign for it.

Unlike banks, credit unions are not protected by the FDIC. However, they are covered by the National Credit Union Share Insurance Fund (NCUSIF), which provides federal and most state-chartered credit union members with up to $250,000 of insurance per individual depositor, per federally insured credit union.

Small Business Association

The Small Business Association (SBA) has a variety of business loans, as well as information to help entrepreneurs get started. Founded in 1953, they have provided vital business information to scores of entrepreneurs and "millions of loans, loan guarantees, contracts, counseling sessions and other forms of assistance to small businesses." The 7(a) Loan

---

▶ Plan Pointer

Lenders look for borrowers exhibiting the four Cs of credit:

1. Character: What's your reputation and background?

2. Capacity or cash flow: Do you have sufficient cash flow to repay principal and interest?

3. Capital: Does your business have enough capital to keep going if you can't pay the debt from earnings?

4. Collateral: Do you own something valuable the banker can take if you can't pay the loan back? Hint: Don't put up your home as collateral.

Program, has become the most popular of their various loans offered. Visit the SBA at www.sba.gov, or www.sba.gov/loanprograms to go directly to their loan information.

Wrap-Up

▶ The well-developed business plan has been called a blueprint for success. It is a valuable tool that can be used to obtain financing and to communicate your goals and objectives to employees.

▶ Financing the business can be achieved through a combination of equity and debt.

▶ Equity investors range from friends and family to venture capitalists and angel investors.

▶ Lenders are most likely banks but can also be credit unions or the Small Business Association (SBA).

Law and the G-Man

Title 26 of the Federal Code, also referred to as the Internal Revenue Code, is made up of 20 volumes and is nearly 17,000 pages long. It includes laws covering income taxes, payroll taxes, gift taxes, estate taxes, and excise taxes. Most states have their own tax regulations covering similar taxes and tack on rules and regulations covering items like workers' compensation insurance and sales taxes. In addition, agencies such as the Social Security Administration and the Equal Employment Opportunity Commission issue their own pamphlets regulating employers. Employer compliance with the myriad of rules and regulations is a daunting task but one that cannot be ignored. A properly established and organized business can cope with the government bureaucracy fairly easily if it understands the basic rules and establishes internal procedures for following those rules.

Business Structure

The first task in setting up your own contracting business is to decide exactly what form, in legal terms, you want your business to be. This legal structure largely determines how much risk the owner takes on and how the government will treat his income. As an entrepreneur you should consult with your lawyer and accountant when deciding which form of business to use, and when consulting with these professionals, be sure to disclose all of your family assets and income, because these factors may influence their recommendations. The choices that business owners have when forming a new company follow:

1. *Sole proprietor.* This form of business has no separate structure from its owner. Even though the sole proprietor may register a trade name like "Jane's Drywall Service," all assets, debts, tax liabilities, and risks belong to Jane. Sole proprietorship has several disadvantages. It may be harder to obtain financing, and you will have unlimited liability in the event the business is sued. This is the simplest form of business and is reserved for the individual entrepreneur. The advantages of being a sole proprietor are being able to make all of the business decisions yourself and sell the business when you choose. There are also few legal costs, little paperwork, no formal business requirements, and no corporate tax payments.

2. *Partnership.* Formed when two or more individuals enter an agreement to manage a business, a partnership does not protect the individual liability of the owners. The partners manage the business and are personally liable for debts and obligations of the business. Like an S corporation (see below), the partnership does not pay taxes because the profits and losses are passed on directly to the partners. From a legal perspective, partnerships are easy to form. Many partnerships are very successful if the partners have a strong bond and their strengths complement each other.

3. *Limited liability company (LLC).* Increasingly popular, this is a hybrid structure that combines the limited liability of a corporation (S or C) with the tax advantages and flexibility of a partnership. The company is owned by members, as opposed to stockholders, and profits and losses are passed on directly to them. In some cases, a

member may contribute services rather than money and, in turn, receive an interest in profits and losses.

4. *S corporation.* Usually reserved for smaller companies with fewer than 100 shareholders, an S corporation provides limited personal liability to its shareholders (owners) so that if the corporation is sued, the personal assets of the shareholders are protected from the lawsuit. The other significant issue with S corporations is that the corporation itself does not pay income taxes. All profits and losses are passed through to the individual shareholders according to the share of the stock each owns. Shareholders are liable for taxes even if they did not receive cash income from the company. The company itself is managed by a board of directors that appoints officers to take responsibility for day-to-day operations.

5. *C corporation.* Most large companies in the United States are C corporations. Like an S corporation, shareholders are protected from lawsuits and the company is managed by a board of directors. However, the corporation is an entity unto itself, which is taxed on its profits, and the shareholders are taxed on any dividends they receive. Shareholders must be aware that dividends are paid on after-tax profits, which results in double taxation because the shareholders are also personally liable for taxes on the dividends they receive.

When deciding on a business structure that meets both your business and personal needs, the entrepreneur should consider the following:

▶ *How vulnerable is your business to lawsuits?* Court dockets are full of suits against contractors. Is your specialty among those involved in numerous lawsuits by unhappy clients? If it is, then a corporation or LLC is the best for you.

▶ *Do you need to pull cash or capital out of the business?* Once you set up a corporation, you cannot generally take money out of it (even if it is your own money) without paying income taxes on the distribution.

▶ *Tax implications are another factor and should be discussed with your accountant.* For example, if you use a company vehicle for personal use, you may have to report the value of the personal use as additional income and pay additional taxes.

▶ *The level of control you want to have over business operations should be discussed with your lawyer.* Corporations are managed by a board of directors and must make financial reports to stockholders. For very small companies, these boards may comprise of only family members. But as the business grows, nonfamily members often join the board, and outsiders may invest in the company. They may also have a say in how your business is run. For greater control, you may be better with a sole proprietorship or partnership if you and your partner agree on who makes decisions on each area of the business.

▶ *The size and nature of the business also influences the structure.* Small companies that focus on limited services may be better run as sole proprietors or LLCs. Among these might be excavating contractors or roofing companies. However, large companies that require large amounts of capital, may have union employees, work on numerous projects at one time, and hire subcontractors usually benefit from a corporate structure.

Accounting Methods

There are two types of accounting methods that are used by small businesses: cash accounting and accrual accounting. The IRS has placed some restrictions on the use of the cash method, so the new contractor is advised to consult with his accountant to decide which is best for his business. While most accounting software programs use the accrual method, it is usually a simple matter for a good accountant to make the year-end adjustments needed to prepare an accurate tax return based on a cash accounting system.

The difference between the two methods is basically one of timing. When using the cash method, revenue is recognized and recorded on the company books when the money is actually received, and expenses are recognized when payment is made. However, when using the accrual method, revenues and expenses are recorded when incurred. Consider the following information:

K&K Contractors—Cash Accounting vs. Accrual Accounting

▶ December 7, 2015: Materials are purchased on credit by K&K for Smith project: $2,500

▶ December 10, 2015: Smith project is completed

▶ December 12, 2015: Smith is sent an invoice for $5,000

▶ December 31, 2015: Tax year ends for K&K Contractors

▶ January 7, 2016: Smith pays $5,000 to K&K

▶ January 30, 2016: $2,500 is paid by K&K to the supplier for Smith materials

The effect on the income statement of K&K Contractors varies by the accounting system used:

1. *Cash accounting.* Neither the $2,500 expense nor the $5,000 income is included in the 2015 income statement because the actual payment and receipt took place in 2016.

2. *Accrual accounting.* Both the $2,500 expense and the $5,000 income are included in the 2015 income statement even though the cash was not received until January 7 and the expense not paid until January 30.

As you can see, the accounting method used can have an effect on your taxes, both positive and negative. Both methods, however, offer legal strategies for accelerating expenses so that they occur in the current year and for deferring income into the following year. Obviously, care must be taken, and consultation and advice from your accountant is paramount.

Bankers, Lawyers, Accountants, and Insurance Agents

These specialists are crucial to a new business. However, although they may be experts in their own field, they may not really understand how your business operates. In order to profitably use their intelligence and expertise, the new business entrepreneur must work closely with these professionals; it is usually a mistake to turn a task over to one of them and think "It's OK, the accountant is handling it." In particular, tax and labor laws are extremely confusing and are subject to a certain amount of interpretation. Also these laws often change. The business owner must help the lawyer and accountant interpret the myriad rules and regulations as they pertain to her specific contracting business.

A good relationship with a banker can both save money and enable to company to operate more smoothly. When looking for a bank to do business with, take along your business plan, or send a copy in advance of your meeting, so that the bank can better understand your goals and objectives and how you will reach them. When a personal business banker understands the financial status of the business and the owners, he is in a good position to advise the company in a number of areas. Because many businesses borrow money from banks to purchase tools and equipment, the banker is a valuable resource for understanding interest rate trends and projections. Again, presenting a clear business plan assists in obtaining loans with the most favorable terms. The banker can also help establish a line of credit for companies that need ongoing cash to support daily operations.

The final outside professional that contractors must have on their team is the insurance agent. Insurance has become a highly complex and specialized business covering all aspects of American life. Three areas of insurance are of particular interest to contractors: 1) general business and vehicles, 2) workers' compensation, and 3) health insurance.

Rather than working with a single insurance company, it is often advantageous to work with an insurance agent who represents a number of different insurance companies. The agent can compare prices to ensure that the contractor is getting the best coverage at the best cost. Often, contracting companies will work with one agent to handle business, vehicle, and workers' compensation and another agent for health insurance. In this age of specialization, other agents may be engaged to find life insurance or long-term health insurance coverage if these are benefits that a business owners wishes to offer his employees.

Coping with the Government

No matter what your political views may be, all business owners must deal with government rules and regulations. Most contractors don't like it but have little choice except to cope as best they can. Certainly lawyers, accountants, bankers, and insurance agents can assist in the process, but the responsibility of complying with the numerous government rules and ordinances falls squarely on the business owner's shoulders. Even though following government guidelines can be difficult, especially when rules and regulations are constantly changing, it is important for the contractor-owner to realize that ignorance of laws is never an excuse for noncompliance. Below are some of the common obligations that businesses face. Fortunately, most of the information on such obligations can be found on the internet at www.irs.gov. The accounts and/or forms that most new businesses must use to operate legally are:

warning

Most contractors have inland marine insurance, which covers equipment other than vehicles. Premiums for this insurance may be based on either replacement cost, which will pay for new equipment to replace destroyed or stolen equipment, or on actual value, which is based on the current depreciated value of the equipment. Actual value insurance has much lower premiums than replacement cost insurance; however, the ultimate cost of replacing equipment is higher. Actual value insurance is usually recommended unless a contracting company generally works in unsafe neighborhoods.

- ▶ Federal government
  - – Employer Identification Number (EIN) (used for income tax forms, it is similar to an individual's Social Security number)
  - – Federal unemployment (Form 940)
  - – Income tax withholding, Social Security, Medicare (Form 941)

- Employee income tax reporting (W-2)
- Employer summary of W-2s (W-3)
- Employee withholding form (W-4)
- Employee proof of citizenship (I-9)
- Dividend or similar payments (1099) (actually, at last count, there are 16 different 1099 forms)

▶ State government

Each state has its own forms and regulations; following is a general list:

- State unemployment
- State income tax withholding
- Workers' compensation (they call it insurance, but in reality it's a tax)
- New hire reporting
- Sales and use tax: state, county, city, stadium
- Professional licenses (architect, surveyor, landscape architect, and engineer, to mention a few)
- Work permits for employees under the age of 18
- USDOT Number for operation of commercial vehicles; varies by state; visit the Federal Motor Carrier Safety Administration at www.fmcsa.dot.gov for more information.

▶ Employee or Contractor?

Following are IRS questions for determining an employee or a contractor. Facts that provide evidence of the degree of control and independence fall into three categories:

1. Behavioral: Does the company control or have the right to control what the worker does and how the worker does his or her job?

2. Financial: Are the business aspects of the worker's job controlled by the payer? (These include things like how the worker is paid, whether expenses are reimbursed, who provides tools/supplies, etc.)

3. Type of Relationship: Are there written contracts or employee-type benefits (i.e., pension plan, insurance, vacation pay, etc.)? Will the relationship continue and is the work performed a key aspect of the business?

Of course, as is always the case with the IRS, you can find a lot more on this very important topic at www.irs.gov.

Employees or Subcontractors

While you may start out as a one-person show, chances are you will soon start hiring employees or start working with subcontractors. It's important that you know the difference, as it matters to the IRS. There are a few key differences between employees and contractors. For example, you control all the jobs and provide the materials for the jobs your employees are responsible for completing. You also take out money for all taxes, Social Security, Medicare, and workers' compensation and pay unemployment insurance. They also represent your business, receive regular payment, and can receive benefits if you offer them. Subcontractors, however, are in control of their own overall work schedule, they can work for other contractors, clients, or companies, and they provide their own tools. They set their own payment terms, use invoices and are responsible for all of their own taxes, Social Security contributions, and benefits.

The determination has implications for your tax liabilities as well as your obligations and commitment to the individual worker. It also determines whether he or she is entitled to benefits such as unemployment and industrial insurance.

Employee Benefits

Providing benefits such as health or retirement plans to employees, including owners, requires additional paperwork and reporting. This is an area where it is very important to work closely with your lawyer and accountant. The rules and regulations covering such benefits are complex and difficult to decipher. Three of the most common benefits are 1) use of a company-owned vehicle, 2) retirement plans such as 401(k), and 3) medical reimbursement plans, or health benefits. Each is governed by its own Internal Revenue Service rulings. Business owners should be aware of each ruling, how it may affect taxable income, and what type of record keeping is required.

An employee may use a company vehicle for personal use, including daily commuting; however, the value of the personal use is included as taxable income for the employee. An employee who uses a company vehicle must keep records that substantiate the portion spent for business use, for which mileage is deductible, and the portion spent for personal use, which is not deductible.

Optional retirement plans have become much easier to administer in recent years. Typically, an employee elects to have a portion of his pay deducted and invested in a mutual fund or other investment. The company can match the employee's contribution up to a limit set by the IRS.

As of 2015, the employee's contribution limit is $18,000 per year, or an additional catch-up contribution of $6,000 for employees age 50 and over at the end of the calendar year. The combined contribution for employee and employer as of 2015 is $53,000, or $59,000 for those using the catch-up plan.

There are other limits on 401(k) plans for highly compensated employees earning over $120,000 (as of 2015). These should be discussed with your plan administrator.

You can find a guide to 401(k) plans at money.cnn.com/retirement/ as well as at the Department of Labor, which has 401(k) information for your business at www.dol.gov/ebsa/publications/401kplans.html. You might also visit http://401khelpcenter.com for more information.

Depending on the type of retirement plan, the amount contributed may be deducted from the employee's taxable income; the company's contribution is generally tax free. Most startup companies are not typically in a position to match such contributions. Also, since you may be working with a lot of subcontractors, you may not have a lot of regular employees, at least not for a while.

Health Plans Can Offer Tremendous Benefits

The most recent health care laws require you to provide certain information about the health care options to your employees whether or not you offer health care. According to the Affordable Care Act , if you offer health insurance to your employees you must offer it within the first 90 days of the first day of employment.

Knowing the health care law is very important for a small business owner especially if you want to offer such health insurance. In a competitive marketplace, you will be able to attract and hire more skilled professionals if you can offer health insurance options.

Documentation and Receipts

While you can store a wealth of data on computers and online "cloud" services, it's still important to have a paper trail to back up the computer data. According to the IRS, a

▶ Small Business Tax Credits

If you have fewer than 25 employees, with an average wage of less than $50,000 per person, you might be eligible for a tax credit if you provide heath insurance to your employees. Check this out at www.irs.gov or put "Small Business Tax Credits" in your online search engine and research the results.

tip

Proof of payment of an amount, by itself, does not establish that you are entitled to a tax deduction. You should also keep other documents, such as credit card slips, invoices, and employee time cards to show that you also incurred the cost.

business must retain records for "as long as they may be needed for the administration of any provision of the Internal Revenue Code." Fortunately the IRS does give some guidance on this issue on its website; as long as the business does not file fraudulent reports, most records can be discarded after seven years.

State governments have their own sets of record-keeping guidelines. For example, the Wisconsin Department of Revenue Sales Tax Division routinely audits businesses to ensure that they are collecting and remitting the proper amount of tax. Its audit usually covers four years; however, it can request records for earlier years if it finds fraudulent activity during the initial audit period.

Record keeping is also useful to a business for its own internal uses. As mentioned earlier, keeping records related to employee benefits is of utmost importance. These items are often red flags for government auditors; a well-organized set of records documenting and justifying benefits will usually save a company time and money in the event of an audit.

Employee performance records are also important because segments of the contracting industry have fairly high employee turnover and relatively high rates for unemployment compensation. An employee who is fired or laid off is usually eligible to receive unemployment benefits, but if an employee is fired because of violations of company policy, he may be ineligible for benefits. However, in order for denial of benefits, the employer must keep a written record of the violations of company policy. These may include unexcused absences, repeated tardiness, or failure to follow safety procedures. Chapter 9 covers the importance of an employee handbook that sets out company policy.

The best approach to record keeping is to be prepared for the audit that may never come. The actual chances of being audited by the IRS are slim. However, it is better to be safe than sorry because audits are very time-consuming and can be expensive. Most businesses can, however, expect an annual audit by their workers' compensation insurance carrier. This compulsory insurance protects employees against loss of income and supplies medical payments if they are hurt on the job.

stat fact

Good news on the audit front! The IRS, like so many businesses, is also having budget woes, and as a result in 2014 large corporations as well as small businesses saw significantly fewer audits.

Because the premiums are based on total payroll, the insurance companies perform an audit every year. Be sure to correctly record employee overtime costs; a portion is exempt from workers' compensation. Therefore, a business owner must keep records of payroll for each job classification in the organization. Failure to keep accurate records can result in overpayment of premiums.

Wrap-Up

save

Know the ins and outs of your state! Some states exempt very small employers from carrying workers' compensation; other states exempt owners who hold more than 25 percent of the stock of the company. Other states cap the amount of income of owners that is taxed. Learn the regulations in your state, and save yourself some money.

▶ The business structure you select will have an important impact on the amount of taxes you pay, the amount of personal risk you assume, and the level of control you have over your business. Careful consideration, in consultation with your lawyer and accountant, must be made prior to choosing a legal structure.

▶ The "government" may seem like a huge monster lurking in the shadows waiting to pounce on the unsuspecting business owner. However, with careful organization and proper accounting, it is relatively easy to satisfy the tax requirements of both state and federal governments. Ignorance of the law is no excuse for violating the rules.

▶ It is important to understand the difference between an employee and a subcontractor for several reasons, especially when it comes to the IRS.

▶ Even if you are not providing health insurance, the new health laws require that you provide such information to your employees. Providing decent health care benefits can give you a leg up on your competition when hiring top candidates.

▶ Maintaining good records is critical to all business enterprises. It is far better to be prepared for the government or insurance audit that may never come.

It's Moving Day

So here we are in Chapter 5, "It's Moving Day," the time to make the big step toward success. At this point, entrepreneurs should have a clear under-standing of the basic foundation needed to start a business.

▶ They understand what a contracting business is and why it is important to the community and the economy.

► They know if they have the proper background, credentials, and personality to become successful.

► They have carefully researched and prepared a business plan and know how they will finance their enterprise.

► They have established relationships with and have consulted with their lawyer, accountant, banker, and insurance agent.

► They understand the requirements that must be met to satisfy state and federal government agencies. They've obtained the licenses they need and have established the required government accounts.

Open Your Office and Shop

One of the first questions startup business owners ask themselves is, "Where should I set up my operations, and how much space do I need?" Many start in their own homes, either in the basement, a spare room, or in the garage. There are certain advantages to starting this way but also many problems.

The positive aspects are largely related to costs. It's cheap. The structure is already there so you have no initial costs to construct or rent a building. You may have some remodeling to do, but most often this can be done at a reasonable cost. There are no rental expenses to pay every month and no landlord to deal with. It's also very convenient to have your office at your home; no time is wasted commuting. Property maintenance and utility costs can be shared by the homeowner (you) and your business. Finally, home improvement expenses such as a new roof can, in part, be treated as a business expense. Many people in all kinds of businesses have found ways to work from a home base.

Now for the downside: The Internal Revenue Service has very strict rules regarding in-home offices, so watch your deductions carefully. You can deduct only that portion of your home, and even your utilities, used for business.

Family support is a crucial factor in deciding to run your business from your home. Because you can never really get away from the office, it's easy to spend too much time at work. Conversely, it is also easy to turn on the television set and get away from work. The key is to be disciplined and manage your time effectively.

save

State governments have a significant influence on businesses. Some states, as well as cities, are particularly friendly to small businesses. As of 2015, the five friendliest small business states were Texas, New Hampshire, Utah, Louisiana, and Colorado. The five friendliest small business cities of 2015 were Manchester, NH; Dallas, TX; Richmond, VA; Austin, TX; and Knoxville, TN.

There are other things to think about when considering a home office. It's important to be able to have a normal home life as well as a stimulating and successful business environment. Ask yourself these questions before you open an office in your home:

▶ Do you have employees who will work full time in your home? How does your family feel about it?

▶ Do you expect to meet with clients at your home? If you do not have a separate entrance to your office, how do your spouse and children feel about strangers walking through their home?

▶ Will the neighbors complain about increased truck traffic stopping to deliver supplies? Will they be upset if you have several trucks and vans parked in your driveway each night?

▶ Do you have enough space to store all your equipment and supplies?

▶ Do local zoning codes allow business activity in your neighborhood? You may also run up against people in home associations or on condo or co-op boards who may give you a hard time about running a business from your home. There may not really be any problem, but typically most people running co-op or condo boards have an ax to grind.

▶ How well are you insured and covered in case a co-worker or client gets injured?

Space: The Next Frontier

No matter where you ultimately decide to open up shop, you must decide how much space you'll need to operate efficiently. As is usually the case, when you think you have just the perfect size office, it will instantly become too small. Ideally, an office should be designed with some flexibility. Most businesses add staff over time and need space for each individual to perform his duties. At a minimum, contractors should have space for the owner, the staff, and a meeting room.

The office for the chief executive of the company should be large enough to hold meetings with at least several people. However, today many meetings include people on conference calls or video conferencing. Off-site meetings have become very easy and often quite cost effective, rather than trying to travel to various meeting locations. In your office search, you need to look at renting spaces that are large enough for a desk, computer, printer, filing cabinet, and perhaps a comfortable chair.

The work space for design staff should be determined by the equipment they use. The drafting table is rapidly becoming a relic as most new designers and architects work on a personal computer. However, they may need space to print out plans and a table to lay them out. Storage space for the printed designs is critical and usually takes up lots of space.

A small conference or meeting room for getting together with clients and sales representatives or holding staff meetings is essential to many businesses in the contracting industry. Some interior designers have suggested that meeting rooms should be designed so that each person attending the meeting has 30 to 35 square feet of space; therefore, if you anticipate meetings with two to six people, a 12 by 16 room should be adequate. If you do not find affordable office space with a large enough meeting area, or conference room, keep in mind that many cities and communities have meeting spaces available for rental. Regus (at www.regus.com) offers meeting rooms and offices in hundreds of cities as well, as virtual offices.

Storage space is often overlooked when planning a new office. Office supplies, machinery, and financial data archives take up quite a bit of room. In addition, most offices have spaces for coffee makers, microwave ovens, and book shelves for industry-specific publications. Of significant concern is having enough outlets for computers and other equipment as well as wifi and/or other means of online connectivity. Make sure you can connect from any place in your office.

Office Specifications and Details

Now that you've got a place for your stuff, you have to decide what that stuff is. A well-stocked and organized office runs much smoother and more successfully than one in a continual state of disarray. If good organization is not a strong suit of a contractor-owner, then she should consider hiring an experienced office manager or executive assistant to keep the office and support staff working smoothly and efficiently. Some of the physical items every contracting office should have follow.

Communications I

The ability to communicate clearly and promptly with both co-workers and clients is critical to any business, especially a contracting business, so the first order of business is installing a telephone system that meets the needs of the business. You should have a landline with an answering machine and a professional greeting.

Ultimately, as an office evolves, a PBX (private branch exchange) system may be necessary. These sophisticated systems, usually costing several thousand dollars, provide a network within an office that offers automatic answering, call transfer, individual voice mail, intercom systems, conference calling, the ability to forward calls to another location, and to make telephone calls over the internet (referred to as VoIP, or Voice over Internet Protocol). Typically, these systems offer callers menu options for their calls: By pressing a series of numbers, the caller can be transferred directly to the person or department sought.

While a PBX telephone system increases the efficiency and usually the professional image of a company, care must be used when relying on one. Many potential clients are turned away by menu options; most people prefer speaking to a "real, live person." They become impatient or angry when forced to listen to a long list of instructions and options. You want to make it as easy as possible for customers and/or potential customers to reach you. The first call a potential client makes is often his introduction to the company, so the method of greeting is crucial. A poor first impression can easily turn away potential clients. A simple answering machine message, having someone (or a service) answer your calls, or having them forwarded to you on your cell phone (if you will be available to take calls) are all possibilities. Most significantly, if you get a phone message, you should respond promptly, within an hour or two.

Communications II

Over the last few years smartphones have all but taken over the world. They are now sophisticated enough to serve as a mobile business control center. Along with the obvious voice services and texting, you have email, web browsing, cameras, and an MP3 player at your disposal. Apps can enhance your user experience, but be forewarned that for every valuable app, there are probably 25 that are quite unnecessary for your business needs—so don't get caught up with endless apps.

Nonetheless, the latest features have turned smartphones into mobile computers. In fact, in recent years, surveys have found that more people are using their phones for computers than they are using their laptops or tablets.

Cell phones are valuable tools for businesses of all sizes. At the typical mom-and-pop contracting company, the owner is frequently on a job site all day. At various times over the course of a day or week, the owner must be able to communicate with clients to ensure that work is proceeding properly, with the office for a wide variety of reasons, with suppliers to verify deliveries or order materials, with future clients to schedule meetings, and with an architect or designer to ask questions about the work.

Larger companies also rely on cell phones to coordinate work among several work crews, to locate a piece of machinery that had to be shared by two crews, or to find someone to repair machinery breaks. If the owner is not present on the job site, the cell phone is an invaluable tool for the crew foreman to verify details of an installation or get approval for changing the plans.

Finally, cell phones are a safety tool. In the event of a serious injury on the job, medical help can be called, and the injured worker treated without unnecessary delay.

Websites such as www.myrateplan.com and http://smartphones.specout.com are valuable for comparing cell phone features as well as cell phone plans available in various regions of the U.S. However, it is always better to speak personally with a sales representative who specializes in business needs. A company that needs several cell phones can often negotiate a better price by talking with a salesperson. Remember, Verizon, AT&T, Sprint, T-Mobile, and others are all very competitive, so go for the best deal you can get.

Communications III

Getting the idea? Efficient communications systems are the lifeblood of any business. Every office needs the following machines to streamline communications and make running the business more efficient, and inevitably, more successful:

1. *Telephone answering machine.* Unless your office has a PBX system, this still works. While it is preferable to have a real person answer calls or forward them to your cell phone, an answering machine can be a useful tool for times when the office staff is busy and for evening and weekends.
2. *Fax machine.* Not very popular anymore, so prices are low, but a fax machine can still be useful for ordering materials, sending government and insurance reports, sending and receiving client documents such as proposals and change orders, and ordering office supplies.
3. *Copy machine.* It's invaluable for making duplicate records, printing copies of inter-office memos for distribution, and myriad other uses too numerous to mention.
4. *Multifunction machine.* It can do many of the above tasks from a single source. These versatile machines can be connected to a personal computer and print, scan, fax, and copy documents of all types; they can also be used as stand-alone machines and act as your primary copy machine.

Computers

A simple desktop computer can handle the daily work of the business. A more powerful computer is needed for computer-aided drafting (CAD) work. A laptop notebook, or the newer and smaller netbook computer, can be a useful selling tool, with photographs of completed work available to show prospective clients. Finally, the tablet computers like the iPad offer business owners a portable device capable of connecting to the internet via cellular services or wifi technology. With a myriad of productivity applications available, most business owners can benefit from these computers.

Much to the dismay of some older architects and designers, the computer has replaced the drafting board and T-square as the primary tool for designing property development projects. Not only do computers make it much easier to make changes and revisions to plans, they can create cost estimates for clients and share information with other design or installation professionals.

Finally, connecting the computer to the World Wide Web via the internet has become the modern way of advertising, communicating, and purchasing. There are, however, several cautionary notes about using the computer as a business tool. First, data and information can be lost if the computer breaks down or is damaged by an electrical storm. Therefore, it is critically important to have a good backup program to save records. Indeed, most computer consultants recommend using two sets of backup media such as a flash drive or external hard drive and a third back up that is taken off-site and kept in a secure place. Today, you can also utilize cloud computer backup, which refers to backing up data to a remote server accessed via the internet. Cloud backup data is stored in, and accessible from, multiple distributed and connected resources that make up a cloud. For more on cloud backup, visit www.webopedia.com/TERM/C/cloud_backup.html.

In recent years, options for online data storage have grown considerably. Check out www.toptenreviews.com for online backup services reviews to research available options. While working away on your computer daily, it's easy to forget how many people every day are devastated when vital data is lost because of a computer virus, malfunction, theft, accident, or even an act of nature. Backing up data is essential. In 2005, for example, when Hurricane Katrina hit the city of New Orleans, business owners who used the backup systems at that time were able to restart their companies much faster than those who lost all of their data . . . some of which never recovered and never returned to business.

> **fun fact**
>
> During the early 1950s, the first commercial computer built in the United States, named UNIVAC, occupied more than 350 square feet of office space (about the size of a two-car garage) and had the ability to perform 1,900 operations per second. In 2012, IBM built a much smaller supercomputer named Sequoia capable of performing 16,320,000,000,000,000 calculations per second.

Office Supplies

Every office needs everyday supplies. Your needs will vary depending on the size of your business and your budget. As you look at the list in Figure 5–1, page 54, prioritize your

Office Supplies Checklist

Items	Price
Postage scale	$
Postage meter or stamps	$
Paper for printer, copy machine, and fax machine if you have one	$
Toner or ink cartridges for printer and other technology	$
"Sticky" notes in an assortment of sizes	$
Scratch and telephone message pads	$
Waste baskets	$
Scissors, utility knives, staplers	$
Three-ring binders and file folders	$
Drafting tools	$
Envelopes and stationery with your logo/company name	$
Return envelopes with your address preprinted	$
Wall safe for storing valuable papers, cash, and computer backup disks	$
Digital camera	$
Measuring wheel and 100-foot tape measure	$
Marking paint and long-handled paint gun	$
Business cards	$
Surge protectors for computers	$
Calculators	$
Calendars and/or planners	$
Flash drives	$
Desk organizers	$
Office furniture	$
Fire extinguishers and first-aid kit	$
Coffee machine and microwave (optional)	$
Paper punch	$
Janitorial and bathroom supplies	$
Total Office Supplies Expenditures:	**$**

FIGURE 5–1: **Office Supplies Checklist**
Use this handy list as a shopping guide for equipping your office with supplies (you probably already have some of these).

needs. After you've done your shopping, fill in the purchase price next to each item, and add up your costs to get a head start on estimating your startup costs. Of course, this is not a complete list of supplies that you may need, so tailor it to what you think you will use.

Tools and Equipment

The contracting industry is large and diverse; each segment has its own specialized tools and equipment. Some contractors work most efficiently when they carry their equipment in a van, some need dump trucks, while others rely on pickup trucks with specialized compartments and racks. The same is true for power and hand tools. The best advice we can give is to encourage you to talk with other contractors and ask what they use. Many established successful contractors are more than happy to help a fledgling business get started. Another approach is to stop at job sites and see what other contractors use; of course, if you have been an employee of a contractor and are striking out on your own, you already know which tools and equipment you'll need to get started.

The Bureaucracy

In Chapter 4, we discussed the types of governmental and insurance accounts required of most businesses. Below is a supplemental list of items and accounts each business should have. Much of this information can be found on the internet at http://business.usa.gov.

- ▶ *Labor law posters.* These are required by both the federal and state governments. These explain various rules and regulations established by government agencies such as the Equal Employment Opportunity Commission (EEOC). These posters, which must be placed in an area where all employees can easily read them, can be ordered from government organizations or from the U.S. Department of Labor. Private companies sell all-in-one posters that include all the required information. Some of these include only federal government posters, others cover individual states, and some are a combination of federal and specific state information.
- ▶ *Occupational Safety and Health Administration (OSHA) Form 300.* Log of work-related injury and illness.
- ▶ *OSHA Form 301.* Injury and illness incident report.
- ▶ *OSHA Form 300A.* Summary of work-related injury and illness. This report must be filled out and posted where employees can read it, even if there are no reported work-related injuries or illnesses.
- ▶ *Safety Data Sheets (SMDS) and Material Safety Data Sheets (MSDS).* Forms that contain information and data about chemicals and other hazardous substances.

The forms contain instructions for safe use of a material and procedures for dealing with emergencies. Employers must have the sheets available for employees who may come in contact with hazardous materials. Suppliers of these materials usually provide the sheets upon request.

▶ *Minor's work permit.* Employees under 18 years old must obtain a work permit prior to starting their employment. These workers have limitations placed on them based on their age and the type of work they perform with both federal and state regulations applicable. Contractors must be careful when hiring young employees because strict safety regulations apply to minor workers. For example, young workers can neither operate a circular saw nor assist operations that use a circular saw. These employees also may not work as roofers. Other regulations govern maximum work hours allowed both on a daily and weekly basis and strict limitations on driving vehicles and operating machinery.

Credit Cards

Be very careful with using credit cards. Failure to pay the full amount due each and every month is an extremely expensive mistake. When late fees are added to interest charges, the cost of paying only a portion of the monthly invoice can easily exceed 20 percent of your purchases. Using a credit card can be a very useful tool for a company. However, care should be taken when deciding which employees have the authority to have or use one. The best advice is to keep the list of users to a bare minimum and require that itemized receipts accompany the monthly invoice and each purchase has a legitimate business purpose. Remember, a simple rule of thumb is to use a credit card by choice as a convenience to help maintain your cash flow or to keep from carrying a lot of cash, but NOT in a situation where you do not have the money available in hopes it will come along later. Remember, debt should be a decision, not a default, and credit card debt is dangerous.

Supplier Credit

Positive cash flow is often a problem for new businesses. During a project, funds are spent on wages and

warning

A construction, or mechanic's, lien is used to collect past due amounts owed to a company claiming the lien. These liens can be attached to land, buildings, or partially completed new construction. Once a lien is placed on property, the owner may lose some control over it until the lien has been satisfied and the past due amounts paid in full. Lien laws vary widely from one state to another and can be very complicated. Understanding how the lien law works in your state may save you money, time, and embarrassment.

materials. Many times a client is not presented an invoice for the work until completion of the project and then may wait 30 days, or longer, to pay the bill. By securing credit with suppliers, a contractor can ease the pressure on cash flow—the money that comes in and out of the bank account. If managed properly, a contractor can purchase materials and often pay for them 30 to 60 days later. While some suppliers request payment in ten days, most do not charge a late fee until the invoice is more than 30 days past due. Every effort must be made to pay supplier invoices on time; and when cash is tight and payments cannot be made on time, the contractor must contact the supplier and explain the situation. Most suppliers are cooperative, especially if the contractor has a good payment record. Still, there are other suppliers who "go by the book" and do not agree to the delay of payment; some will even send a notice to your client that they will place a lien on his property if payment is not made. For obvious reasons, contractors must avoid this scenario at all cost.

Banking

Most contracting businesses require at least two types of bank accounts for handling their cash: a checking account, which does not pay interest, for accounts payable and payroll, and a savings or money market account for holding excess cash until it is needed. Interest rates for these types of accounts vary and change as the national economy changes, but the rates have been rather low in recent years. As a new business owner, however, you are not in a position to take on any high-risk investments with your profits.

Using cash as a vehicle to pay suppliers or employees is a very poor way of doing business. It also makes record-keeping difficult and opens the door to abuse and even theft. Instead, checks, credit, and credit cards are far better and safer methods of spending money. Online banking makes it very easy to handle your banking transactions and keep track of your balance at all times. Most banks have made online banking very easy in recent years.

Start Me Up

Many entrepreneurs start their own business because they do not want to work at repetitive or boring jobs. Factory work has no appeal to them. They cannot imagine sitting behind a desk eight hours a day, shuffling papers. Spending days in a retail store is abhorrent to their senses. They are looking for work that is not routine and varies from day to day. The contracting industry offers just the type of working atmosphere that these entrepreneurs want and enjoy.

If you were to ask a contractor to describe a typical day at work, he would tell you that there is no such thing. That's not to say that each of the 60 or 70 hours you will work each week is thrilling and rewarding. Every job has its unpleasant moments, and the contracting industry is no exception. However, for a vast majority of successful contractors, the fun times on the job far outnumber the frustrating and unpleasant times.

Most contractors start their days well before 7 A.M., when they begin to review the schedule for the day. While they usually have a schedule for the week on their iPhone or organizer, disruption and changes are the norm. Here are a few such business disruptions to explain why contractors must remain flexible:

- ▶ Poor weather can cause a situation where even if you can get onto the job site, your work would not be productive.
- ▶ An employee or several employees call in sick.
- ▶ Supplies ordered for a job have been delayed in shipment.
- ▶ The supplier has sent the wrong materials.
- ▶ Equipment breakdown; a spare is not available.
- ▶ The client has changed his mind and wants to review the plans before more work is done.
- ▶ A subcontractor has not completed her work or has to alter work already completed.
- ▶ Your computers or wifi is down.

Experienced entrepreneurs appear to have an instinctive ability to "see the big picture" and understand that the various elements of their business must work harmoniously for the business to succeed. However, the importance of attending to the smallest detail cannot be stressed enough. Entrepreneurs who are able to set effective company policies and passionately communicate their vision for success but overlook or ignore seemingly mundane details, such as meeting financial deadlines or following through on promises to employees or customers, are likely heading down the road to failure. This is not to imply that owners should micro-manage their business, but they must convey the importance of "attention to detail" to their employees.

Many new contractors wear multiple hats. They are the employer, the workforce, the scheduler, the mechanic, the designer, the bookkeeper, and the salesperson. While a spouse or partner may be of great assistance with these tasks, the owner usually has to spend a portion of his day on one or more of these tasks. Orders for materials have to be reviewed, customer statements have to be verified, equipment must be maintained, and new business secured. Most often, a contractor will work in the field during the day, spend a few hours in the late afternoon or early evening meeting with prospective clients, and then head back to the office to take care of paperwork and make telephone calls.

Saturdays are much the same, except more time may be spent on equipment maintenance, paperwork, and communications with clients. The weekend typically becomes Saturday night and all day Sunday. With disruption and chaos constantly lurking in the background, it is vital that contractors remain flexible enough to "change horses in midstream" and be nimble enough to remain productive when the expected work schedule is changed.

One of the keys to success for contractors is learning how to efficiently schedule your labor and to manage the productivity of your work crews. It makes no difference if you are a one-person outfit or have 30 employees; productivity of labor must be constantly maintained even when all or some of the factors listed above are threatening to bring your workday to a screeching halt.

A contractor does not generate income for every hour he or she works. Time spent on the telephone, returning emails, or calling on a prospective client is not what some lawyers call "billable hours." Contractors can rarely send a bill to a client who calls to ask questions about her project, and time spent preparing government reports cannot be billed to anyone.

The contractor must become something of a juggler when family or personal situations arise that require absence from work. Your teenage son's championship soccer game is scheduled for 3 P.M. on Thursday; your daughter is starring in the school play scheduled for 1 P.M. on Wednesday; your spouse wants you to take the kids away for a few days to the new water park; your doctor has scheduled some tests for 9 A.M. Monday morning. For the very small contractor, these obligations do not pose a huge problem. Many clients understand that contractors actually have lives besides their work and are agreeable when you inform them in advance that you'll not be on the job during those hours. But you must remember that during these times you are not generating income. Part of running a business is working to grow that business for the future.

Missing work is more difficult for the medium-sized contractor who has just a few employees. When you take time off to tend to personal obligations, your field workers may be left without proper supervision. Therefore, proper planning for the productivity of your work crew becomes a critical issue. Before an owner can send a field employee to a job site unsupervised, she must be confident that the employee has the knowledge and ability to complete the tasks satisfactorily. As some employees learn faster than others, the owner must be able to take whatever time is necessary to properly train each individual. Your goal should be to have a business that will not fall apart if you are not there. As a business grows you will hopefully find enough quality people so that if you are out sick or even go on vacation, these trusted individuals can keep everything running smoothly.

'Tis the Season

Some specialties in the contracting industry face unique challenges as a result of geographical location and weather. In the southwestern regions of the United States, extreme heat during the summer may limit the amount of physical activity that workers should do. Many who live there might say "It's hot, but it's dry heat." However, if it is 115 degrees, it's still hot. Employees working under these conditions should receive training to limit the risks of working in hot weather, to recognize the symptoms of the onset of heat exhaustion or heat stroke, and to learn what steps they should take if they or a co-worker becomes disabled due to heat stroke.

In other areas of the country, particularly in the north, contractors face obstacles created by adverse weather during the winter months. When the ground is frozen, excavators, landscape contractors, and even plumbers may not be able to work on a consistent basis. Some may have to lay off employees and reduce their staff to a bare minimum.

In recent years, however, many of these northern businesses have offered new services in order to maintain a revenue stream. Two of the most popular are snow removal and holiday decorating. Some have sold Christmas trees, others might provide carpet-cleaning services during the winter and/or repair snowmobiles.

Innovative entrepreneurs consider all their options, examine the costs and benefits they expect from a new venture, weigh the strengths and weaknesses of their staff, and forge ahead with the new service. Clients will expect the same high level of performance that is provided by your regular services. Therefore, employees must be properly trained to perform the tasks required by the seasonal service; substandard work will backfire and hurt the reputation of the company as a whole. Consider your skills and those of your employees, and see if you can forge another source of income during the down months in your business.

Wrap-Up

▶ Using your home as an office can be very beneficial to a new contracting business; however, there are disadvantages. Weigh the pros and cons carefully.

▶ Plan your spatial needs before building or renting; most likely, you'll need more space than you think.

► Up-to-date communications systems are crucial to the success of a new contracting business.

► Set a realistic and thorough budget for office supplies and equipment.

► Visit http://business.usa.gov to learn about the variety of government regulations that cover small business.

► Visit your state's website to discover relevant regulations.

► There is no such thing as a typical day in the contracting industry.

► Geographical location may bring special challenges to many contracting businesses. Find ways to work around such challenges so that they do not bring your business to a halt.

► Consider other means of generating income if you are living and working in a part of the country that limits your business activity during certain times of the year.

Financial Techniques for Profitability

B enjamin Franklin once said:

Beware of small expenses;

a small leak will sink a great ship.

While there are numerous reasons why businesses fail,

money woes and financing issues rank near the top, espe-

cially for companies engaged in contracting. Many con-

tractors fail to correctly recognize their true cost of doing business and thus fail to properly price their services accordingly. It is very interesting to know that in the same geographical area of the country, competitive bids for the same work from several contractors can differ by as much as 30 percent. Does this mean that some contractors deliberately overcharge their clients or that others are giving the work away? Absolutely not. There are typically legitimate reasons for a wide variance among bids for the same work. Contractor A, for example, may have a larger, more stable, and more experienced workforce who demand higher wages, while contractor B may work out of his home, have few employees, and thus have very low expenses. However, contractor C may not truly understand and account for all of his expenses and therefore actually undercharge clients.

Contractors who have a reputation for excellent work that is completed on time and within budget are usually able to charge more than the contractor who is late, installs the incorrect product, and adds "extra charges" when the project is completed. This chapter covers the strategies for establishing a budget and how to use it to calculate a fair and profitable price for services. It establishes the framework for Chapter 7, which explains how to use the budget to determine what level of annual revenues is needed to make a profit.

The Tools to Make a Budget

Creating a budget for a new contracting business, or any business, can be a difficult because of the lack of a spending history. Established businesses have years of spending records to help them estimate future spending. Without a track record, a new business must make educated projections based on the best available information and then actively monitor and update its budget as actual spending information is known.

Assistance may be available from a number of sources, including former employers, industry associations, suppliers, and even some competitors. Asking a large competitor for help might seem like a daunting task, but

save

Most software companies offer product upgrades nearly every year. Often, these upgrades offer minor changes to the basic programming. While it is important to keep up to date with the latest software enhancements, money can be saved by upgrading your software every other time it is offered. Study the new features offered by an upgrade, and decide if you can postpone them by a year or so. Caution: If your software becomes obsolete because you skipped too many upgrades, it's probable that the software company will cease providing technical support for your older software.

surprisingly, many large, established companies are eager to help a startup contracting business. They take it as a compliment that someone respects them enough to ask for advice. They have a vested interest in seeing that new businesses in their industry present themselves in a positive light. And, they are so well established that they have few worries about competition from a startup.

The first thing you need to do when considering your budget is make sure you know what you absolutely need in order to make the business work. Often, we have items available that we do not need to buy if we are starting a small one- or two-person operation. For example, in the early stages, your current computer may do the trick, as long as it supports financial and accounting software. In all fairness, budgets can even be made on Microsoft Excel spreadsheets. In fact, some business owners prefer making a simple budget without the complexities found in some software programs. Remember, software is a tool to help you with a budget and with financial matters. You, however, are in charge of the basics, which means knowing how much you are spending and where you are making a profit, or not.

New business owners can save money and keep budget items to a minimum by being creative. Many business owners have used furniture and crates saved in their basements or in the garage as a starting point for their office furnishings and storage.

Accounting Tools

By using accounting software, a contractor can track expenses, both by category and by supplier; organize client information and accounts receivable; manage employee wages, deductions, and benefits; and accurately file government reports and payments. Four of the highest rated accounting programs for small business are FreshBooks (www.freshbooks. com), Sage One (at www.sageone.com), AccountEdge Pro (at http://accountedge.com) and QuickBooks Pro by Intuit, Inc. (at http://quickbooks.intuit.com/). There are versions available for both the PC and Macintosh.

There is another invaluable tool that becomes the heart of the budget-making process—the spreadsheet.

As you will learn later in this chapter, the spreadsheet is helpful with financial management because it can be used to understand the effects of increased or decreased spending. For example, the spreadsheet can be used to answer a question like, "If I hire a salesperson and increase total wages by $25,000, how much will the cost of employee benefits increase and how much more revenue will I need to generate this year to pay for these increased costs? OK, now what happens if the person I hire wants to be paid $35,000?"

All the budget maker has to do is enter either amount of the new wage, and the questions will be automatically answered. It's a great tool for all sorts of "what-if" questions.

Why Set a Budget?

Establishing a budget for your business is a key ingredient to success. A contracting company may have the most skilled employees, the newest equipment, a top-notch sales team, and a creative advertising and marketing program; but failure is destined if the company does not have a comprehensive financial plan. The budget is the first step in creating this plan because it:

- ▶ Helps plan for the future
- ▶ Helps plan and manage your money
- ▶ Helps identify problems before they occur or get out of hand
- ▶ Helps you meet your goals and objectives
- ▶ Improves the decision-making process
- ▶ Increases employee motivation
- ▶ Helps keep costs under control

Although the budget can be considered a road map to financial success, the road is littered with potholes and detours. Never consider your budget to be a fixed document that you prepare once and never change. It is a dynamic document that will undergo revisions and modifications during the year. Most often, these changes will be minor, with little effect on your overall financial plan.

Costs First

Many new business owners begin their budget process by trying to determine what their total revenues will be for the year. They think that by considering revenues first, they'll be in a position to know how much money they can spend during the course of the year. What they often overlook is consideration of how they will achieve the projected revenues. Merely knowing or guessing annual

tip

When establishing a budget, weigh the costs and benefits of your spending decisions. For example, let's say you plan to buy a piece of equipment for $10,000. However, the dealer has another model that is larger, faster, and more efficient at a cost of $14,000. Ask yourself if the additional cost of $4,000 will generate a net benefit to the company of at least that much. If it does, buy the more expensive model. This concept of marginalism shows that additional (marginal) costs and additional (marginal) benefits are pertinent to financial decision making.

revenues does not provide a strategy for pricing your services nor does it instill any kind of spending discipline. Projected revenue is something you cannot necessarily control, since you do not know how many jobs you will get and how much of that revenue may not occur based on factors that are out of your control, ranging from a recession to weather conditions to a major competitor opening in your area of business.

Conversely, spending is something that you can control. You can decide how much you'd like to spend while knowing your minimum needs. Sure you might like a large office space, but you might be better off taking a more realistic approach and budgeting for a moderate-size office.

The budget process begins and ends with a detailed and organized system that projects annual spending in various categories and then uses these spending amounts to determine the amount of revenue needed to pay for the spending, leaving enough at the end of the year for a profit.

Direct Costs

The sample budget used in this chapter will be divided into three distinct categories of expenses, each with its own unique characteristics. The first category contains direct job costs, or just direct costs, expenses specifically related to projects completed by the company. It includes materials, labor, and subcontractors, if any; it also includes the rental of any equipment that might be required to complete the projects.

One of the most difficult concepts for new contractor-owners to grasp is the true cost of labor. An employee earning $10 per hour actually costs his or her employer much more than that. In addition to the hourly wage, the employer incurs costs in the following categories:

▶ Social Security and Medicare taxes
▶ Unemployment taxes, both federal and state
▶ Workers' compensation insurance
▶ Paid holidays and vacations; sick days
▶ Health insurance premiums
▶ Overtime

When you combine these costs, which we call the "labor burden," you'll get a truer picture of your actual cost of doing business. Most businesses have different classes of employees, such as the field laborers who install the projects, the sales force, and the office staff. Each category will have a slightly different calculation for labor burden. For illustration purposes, imagine a contracting company that works 52 weeks per year, has six field laborers, one office worker, and an owner who handles sales, design, and general administration of the business. The charts that follow reflect this imaginary company, K&K Contractors LLC. However, the concepts work well with companies of all sizes and configurations.

When compiling the information needed to complete the calculations, some projections will have to be made. You can never truly know the future, but you can make rational estimates.

Take a look at the Figure 6–1, "Labor Burden Calculation for Field Labor," on page 69. At the top of the chart, total annual regular wages are listed for six employees. The totals are based on a year of 50 working weeks of 40 hours each. The remaining two weeks of the year are reserved for vacation time. Our hypothetical company, K&K Contracting LLC, has a total yearly field payroll of $187,500.

The bottom portion of the chart lists the various taxes and benefits. These are costs that relate directly to the wages of the contracting employees who work at job sites. Office personnel, sales staff, and executives are not included (unless the latter work regularly with the work crews at the job sites).

tip

Hiring subcontractors is a very popular manner of bringing in staff for projects because it saves money in many ways. Not having to pay benefits allows you to pay at a higher hourly rate and still save money. You are also not carrying a higher payroll during slower times of year. Plus you can bring in experts in areas you may not need on an ongoing basis. Look for trustworthy and competent contract employees.

Every contracting company will have a slight variation from this chart; every state has its own rates for unemployment and workers' compensation, and general liability. The various taxes and benefits of K&K Contracting are:

- ► *Social Security and Medicare taxes.* Employers and employees each pay these taxes. The employer's portion for Social Security is 6.2 percent of an employee's wage, up to an annual limit set by the federal government. For 2015, the wage limit was $118,500, meaning that the maximum amount an employer must pay for one employee is $7,347. The employee's portion is 6.2 percent of his or her wage. There is no maximum wage limit for Medicare taxes, which have a rate of 1.45 percent for the employer. Employees pay the same amount, which is deducted from their paychecks and sent to the government by the employer.
- ► *State unemployment tax.* The tax rates are established by individual states and vary widely. Taxes are usually paid by the employer and not deducted from an employee's

Labor Burden Calculation for Field Labor

Total Field Payroll	Hours Worked per Year	Wage Rate	Annual Wage	Explanation of Calculation
3 Foremen	2,000 each, 6,000 total	$18.75	$112,500	$18.75 x 6,000
3 Laborers	2,000 each, 6,000 total	$12.50	$75,000	$12.50 x 6,000
Total annual wage			$187,500	
Labor Burden	**Calculation Parameters**	**Rate**	**Cost**	**Explanation of Calculation**
Social Security/Medicare	percentage of total payroll	7.65%	$14,344	.0765 x $187,500
State unemployment	first $10,000 each employee	5.00%	$3,000	(.05 x $10,000) x 6 employees
Federal unemployment	first $7,000 each employee	0.60%	$252	(.006 x $7,000) x 6 employees
Workers' compensation	percentage of total payroll	9.00%	$16,875	.09 x $187,500
General liability	percentage of total payroll	1.00%	$1,875	.01 x $187,500
Paid vacations	3 foremen @ 2 weeks each		$4,500	$18.75 x 80 hours x 3 foremen
	3 laborers @ 2 weeks each		$3,000	$12.50 x 80 hours x 3 laborers
Paid holidays	7 days for 3 foremen		$3,150	$18.75 x 56 hours x 3 foremen
	7 days for 3 laborers		$2,100	$12.50 x 56 hours x 3 laborers
Health insurance	$150 per month per employee		$7,560	$150 x 6 employees x 12 months x 70% employer contribution
	Employer pays 70%			
Overtime	time-and-a-half over 40 hours per week; estimate 4 hours		$13,500	$18.75 x 1.5 x 4 hrs x 40 weeks x 3 foremen
	per week for 40 weeks per employee		$9,000	$12.50 x 1.5 x 4 hrs x 40 weeks x 3 laborers
Total Labor Burden			**$79,021**	
	Percent of total annual wage		**42.1%**	

FIGURE 6–1: **Sample Labor Burden Calculation for Field Labor, K&K Contracting**

paycheck. Most states have a range of rates, so employers who lay off more employees incur a higher tax rate, which also points in favor of subcontractors rather than a lot of full-time employees. Again, most states have a taxable wage limit; after an employee's annual wage exceeds a certain amount, unemployment taxes are no longer charged to the employer. A few states offer an exemption to certain owners of the business; however, care must be taken with this option as it may result in higher federal unemployment taxes.

▶ *Federal unemployment tax.* This tax is fairly simple and straightforward for most employers. The tax rate, as of 2015, is 6.0 percent of the first $7,000 of each employee's wage, but most employers receive a credit of 5.4 percent when they file their Form 940, resulting in a net tax of 0.6 percent, or $42 per year.

▶ *Workers' compensation.* Once again each state has its own laws governing workers' compensation insurance, which provides coverage for employees who are injured on the job. While the states set the rates, usually in dollars per $100 of payroll, insurance companies sell the product. These insurance companies are in competition and can offer to pay a dividend (return of premium) to companies who have excellent safety records. Rates in contracting and construction are typically very high due to the risk of injury on job sites. However, dividend payments can be as much as 50 percent of the annual premium.

▶ *General liability.* The premiums for this insurance are based on payroll and vary from state to state and from contractor to contractor. The insurance covers several items, but the two most important features insure against damage to a client's property and against injury or harm done after a project is completed. For example, if an employee backs a vehicle into a client's garage, the general liability insurance will cover the damage; or if someone trips on a step installed by a contractor, general liability insurance will provide some protection against lawsuits and should pay for repair.

▶ *Paid vacations and holidays.* While these are actually employee fringe benefits, they are expected by most employees. Employers who do not offer these benefits risk losing employees to competing businesses.

▶ *Health insurance premiums.* Health insurance is a hot button-issue these days and is often the single largest annual expense for a small business. The health insurance industry is very complex and in a constant state of change. Therefore, contractors should consult with independent insurance agents who specialize in the field. This is certainly an area where one size does not fit all. Insurance agents can shop around to find the best plan for each contracting company. Typically, employers ask each employee to contribute a portion of the premiums.

▶ *Overtime*. Unless a contractor can charge its clients extra when an employee works more than 40 hours per week, the cost of overtime should be included in the labor burden. In the case of K&K Contracting, each worker is estimated to work 44 hours a week for 40 weeks and 40 hours for the remaining 12 weeks of the year. The federal government has ruled that in general, employers must pay a wage of one-and-one-half times a worker's regular wage for each hour over 40 worked in one week.

warning

Some employees must be paid overtime even if they are paid a salary. The rules are complex, so make sure you understand which of your employees must receive time and a half when they work more than 40 hours in a week.

As we see in Figure 6–1, the total labor burden for K&K Contracting LLC is just over $79,000 per year for its six employees. Therefore, the annual labor costs are far higher than the regular wages paid to employees. But how is this information useful to the budget and estimating process? Simple, really. You calculate the labor burden's cost as a percentage of total field payroll by dividing the labor burden by the total payroll as follows:

$$\$79,239 \div \$187,500 = .421 = 42.1$$

As indicated earlier, labor costs are only one part of direct costs; the remainder includes estimated annual costs for materials, equipment rental, and subcontractors. In Figure 6–2 (page 72), we've set up a hypothetical direct cost budget for K&K Contracting.

Astute readers will notice that the cost of labor listed in the direct cost budget, given in Figure 6–2, ($101,250 + $67,500 = $168,750), does not equal the total annual wage ($187,500) listed on the labor burden worksheet, Figure 6–1. The reason for this is that we are reserving 10 percent of the cost of labor for what is called "yard time," which is the cost of paying employees when they are not on the job sites generating revenues. They may be maintaining equipment, taking part in staff meetings, attending job-related seminars, on break, or performing warranty work. Every company will have its own calculation for yard time. But for the purposes of this book, we'll use 10 percent (about four hours per week, average, per employee).

Therefore, K&K Contractors expects to spend approximately $600,000 for materials and labor that are used expressly for the projects it works on. We'll save this amount for now and come back to this after we set a budget for the other two categories of spending.

Direct Costs Budget for 2XXX

	Annual Expense
ABC Contractors Supply	$85,000.00
Continental Materials	$110,000.00
USA Hardware	$35,000.00
County Builders & Supply	$55,000.00
Jones & Jones Lumber	$30,000.00
All-State-Rent-It-All	$17,500.00
National Plastics	$25,000.00
Foreman's wages	$101,250.00
Laborers' wages	$67,500.00
Labor burden @ 42.1%	$71,043.75
Total Direct Costs	**$597,293.75**

FIGURE 6–2: **A Sample Direct-Cost Budget**

Fixed Costs

Every business has costs that it incurs regardless of the level of business activity. These are amounts due on a regular basis and are fairly constant from one year to the next when adjusted for inflation. Fixed costs include expenditures for items such as:

- ▶ Officer and office salaries
- ▶ Interest expense
- ▶ Rent and utilities
- ▶ Telephone service
- ▶ Advertising and marketing

For example, a company pays a fixed amount of rent each month for its office space regardless of how busy it might be; it signs a lease agreement for $1,000 per month and must pay that amount whether its annual revenues are $100,000 or $2,000,000. However, some fixed costs may "break the rule" and increase more than an increase in revenues. Telephone service is one example: if revenues unexpectedly surge, a company may have to add additional telephone lines to handle the increased business. But for the purposes of this book, assume that fixed costs will remain relatively constant. However, before the fixed cost budget category is set up, the labor burden for the office staff must be determined.

Refer to Figure 6–3 on page 74, which is very similar to Figure 6–1.

You can make the same mathematical calculation used in Figure 6–1 to determine the labor burden as a percentage of total office payroll as shown:

$$\$14{,}769 \div \$75{,}000 = .196 \text{ or } 19.6\%$$

This is much lower than the labor burden for field labor, primarily because workers' compensation rates are much lower for office workers and because holidays, vacations, and overtime are included in the salaries of these workers. Once again, for every $10 that you pay office staff, you'll pay an additional $1.96 to the various state and federal governments and for fringe benefits. Putting together the fixed-cost budget results in Figure 6–4, page 75.

Several items in the fixed cost budget need further explanation and clarification.

save

If you find that your business is growing and you have the opportunity to rent a larger space than you currently need, at a good price, you might elect to go for it and split the space with another company or either lease it or sublet it if it's OK with a landlord.

▶ *Bank payments.* We include both principal and interest paid for the bank loans secured to buy equipment. Since the budget is concerned with actual spending, We'll leave income tax ramifications to the accountant.

▶ *Capital equipment fund.* While this is an optional expense, we strongly recommend establishing a fund to be set to purchase equipment or to make a down payment on a loan for equipment. Companies with very good credit ratings can often secure bank loans for the total purchase price of a piece of equipment. However, by creating a separate capital equipment fund, future principal and interest payments can be reduced, thereby improving the monthly cash flow of the business.

▶ *Other items.* The fixed-cost budget is fairly simple but realistic for a small business. Some other expenses that companies include as fixed-cost budget items are: employer portion of retirement plans, professional expenses such as attendance at trade shows or seminars, as well as advertising and marketing, association dues, and other employee benefits.

▶ *Anticipate.* When compiling the information for your fixed-cost budget, remember to include items that may increase later in the year due to other spending. For example, if you plan to purchase a new vehicle in September, remember to add the cost of insurance for the last four months of the year as well as the cost of the license plate.

Office Staff Labor Burden

Office Payroll	Hours Worked per Year	Wage Rate	Annual Wage	Explanation of Calculation
Owner	salary	$50,000	$50,000	
Assistant	salary	$25,000	$25,000	
Total annual wage			**$75,000**	

Labor Burden	Calculation Parameters	Rate	Cost	Explanation of Calculation
Social Security/Medicare	percentage of total payroll	7.65%	$5,737.50	.0765 x $75,000
State unemployment	first $10,000 each employee	5.00%	$1,000	(.05 x $10,000) x 2 employees
Federal unemployment	first $7,000 each employee	0.60%	$84	(.006 x $7,000) x 2 employees
Workers' compensation	percentage of total payroll	2.00%	$1,500	.02 x $75,000
General liability	percentage of total payroll	1.00%	$750	.01 x $75,000
Paid vacations	Included in salary		$0	
Paid holidays	Included in salary		$0	
Health insurance	Employer pays 70%		$5,670	Owner: $500 per month, assistant: $175 per month
Overtime	None		$0	
Total Labor Burden			**$14,742**	
Percent of total annual wage			**19.6%**	

FIGURE 6–3: **A Sample Analysis of Office Staff Labor Burden for K&K Contractors**

Fixed-Costs Budget for 2XXX

	Annual Expense
Kate's salary	$40,000
Ken's salary	$40,000
Office assistant salary	$24,000
Labor burden @ 19.6%	$20,384
Insurance (building/vehicle)	$3,000
Health insurance (office staff)	$10,000
Telephone	$900
Cell phone plan	$3,000
Online provider	$1,200
Bank payments	$25,000
Capital equipment fund	$5,000
Licenses	$1,200
Utilities	$1,800
Rent	$12,000
Total Fixed Costs	**$187,484**

FIGURE 6–4: **A Sample Fixed-Cost Budget Analysis**

To review, the fixed-cost budget for K&K Contracting amounts to $187,484, meaning that the company expects to spend that much regardless of the amount of revenues that are generated during the year. It is crucial that the fixed-cost budget be realistic and accurate because not only does it impact the pricing of services, it also helps determine the annual revenue required to make a profit. We'll come back to the profit issue later in this chapter.

Variable Costs

The third category of spending is called variable expenses because items here usually change in real terms, or dollar amounts, as the level of business activity increases. In addition, they tend to remain about the same percentage of direct costs. In other words, if direct costs increase from one year to the next by 15 percent, it is likely that as a group variable costs will also rise approximately 15 percent. An example of variable costs is the cost of travel expenses. When business activity increases, a company is more likely to have employees

▶ Depreciation

Did you know that equipment purchases can be depreciated over time, reducing the income tax burden? Depreciation can be a complex concept; we strongly recommend consulting with an accountant in order to receive the most favorable benefit from depreciating equipment.

An excellent way to plan for the future is to prepare a chart listing all of your depreciable equipment, such as vehicles and skid loaders, and projecting the useful life of each. Then estimate the replacement cost, adjusting for inflation. Knowing when and how much you will have to borrow for capital equipment is critical to both the current and future annual budget process. Saving for the future takes good planning and great discipline but is well worth the time and effort.

travel to more work locations for client meetings as well as work on the job. Other items we also include in variable costs are:

▶ Vehicle maintenance and repairs
▶ Office expenses
▶ Office supplies
▶ Printing
▶ Employee incentive or bonus pay
▶ Advertising and marketing
▶ Small tools; hardware
▶ Uniforms
▶ Salesperson salaries and commissions

Some costs overlap between fixed and variable. These include items such as advertising. While the cost of advertising on a website may be constant from one month to the next, advertisements in local newspapers or magazines may be placed at irregular intervals—or not at all. The variable-cost budget for K&K Contracting given in Figure 6–5 on page 77 is fairly easy to understand. These are the costs that will change as business activity changes. We strongly recommend including a budget for "contingency." Unfortunately, you cannot expect the unexpected—as when the United States experienced a

warning

In most states, price fixing of a product or service is illegal. Generally speaking, a company may not, with another company, agree to set a price for a particular product or service. However, conformity of prices for a particular product or service is not illegal unless the conformity was created in combination with other companies agreeing on a set price.

Variable Cost Budget for 2XXX

Miscellaneous expenses	$6,000	
Gasoline/diesel fuel	$10,000	
Advertising	$12,000	special sales, magazine ads, fliers, websites, Yellow Pages, online directories that charge a fee
Postage	$750	
Printing	$1,000	invoice forms, checks, contract forms
Office supplies	$4,000	envelopes, computer supplies, etc.
Hardware store/small tools	$3,000	upkeep of property
Equipment repairs	$10,000	vehicles and equipment
Uniforms	$900	
Employee yard time	$18,750	estimated at 10% of wage cost
Employee incentives	$6,000	employee awards and bonuses
Labor burden @ 42.1%	$10,420	
Cell phones (overage)	$300	
Contingency	$2,000	
Returns	$3,000	warranty work
Total Variable Costs	**$86,120**	

FIGURE 6–5: **A Sample Variable-Cost Budget**

jump in the price of gasoline to $4 per gallon. Employee incentives are in the variable cost budget even though they may not increase as revenues increase. However, they are certainly not fixed costs, and it would be a stretch to include them in direct costs. Because they are usually tied to employee performance, the best place for them is with variable costs.

Overhead

Well, now what? Direct costs, fixed costs, and variable costs are identified as the major components of a budget. This is all well and good, but what does it tell you, and how can you benefit from the knowledge gained from compiling these budget numbers? First it's a valuable exercise that forces a business owner to correctly identify all of the costs of doing business. But more importantly, you can use the information to assist in setting prices for your products and services.

Now that you've identified three categories of spending, the next step is to combine two of them and give them a new name. Each will keep its own identity, but they work together to make what is called "overhead," which is the ongoing general and administrative expenses that are not directly related to the selling of a company's goods and services. To that end, you'll combine fixed costs and variable costs to calculate total overhead expense. Using the example of K&K Contracting, combining these costs gives the following results:

$$\text{Fixed costs} = \$187,484$$
$$+ \text{Variable costs} = \$86,120$$
$$= \text{Overhead} = \$273,604$$

One way to consider overhead is that it supports direct costs. When money is spent specifically to generate revenues (direct costs), money is also spent in the office and elsewhere to support those direct costs. The budget you are developing will help you determine how you will generate revenues to pay for or to recover overhead expenses. The first step is to understand the relationship between direct costs and overhead. Consider this formula:

$$\text{Total overhead} \div \text{Direct costs} = \text{Overhead recovery percent}$$

And when we plug in our numbers:

$$\$273,604 \div \$597,293 = .458 \text{ or } 46\% = \text{Overhead}$$

What this means is that for every $100 spent on direct costs an additional $46 will be spent on overhead. With a little experience, it is fairly easy to determine the cost of materials for a project as well as the time estimated to complete it. Once this is accomplished, the cost of overhead recovery falls right into place.

Alternative Method

Some contractors, either by preference or because the competition demands it, allocate overhead only to their labor costs. In the case of K&K Contracting, when overhead is allocated to labor only, the overhead recovery rate is 114 percent ($273,604 ÷ $239,793). This may be acceptable for some companies, especially if the relationship between materials and labor is relatively constant. However, when the cost of materials is extremely high relative to the cost of labor, the result is usually to undercharge the client. The reverse is usually true when the cost of labor is high relative to the cost of materials.

In Figure 6–6 on page 79, the costs of four separate projects are presented using two different methods. Method A allocates overhead evenly between materials and labor, while Method B allocates overhead to labor costs only. As can be seen by the results, Method B shows no constant relationship to Method A: Differences range from +39 percent to –7 percent.

Overhead Recovery

	Project A	Project B	Project C	Project D
Cost of materials	$50	$50	$5,000	$5,000
Hours to do the job	20	100	20	100
Wage cost @ $15.625				
per hour	$313	$1,563	$313	$1,563
Labor burden @ .421	$132	$658	$132	$658
Wage cost + labor burden	$445	$2,220	$445	$2,220

Method A: Allocate overhead equally to materials and labor				
Materials + labor	$495	$2,270	$5,445	$7,220
Overhead @ 46%	$228	$1,046	$2,505	$3,323
Break-even point	$722	$3,316	$7,949	$10,543

Method B: Allocate overhead to cost of labor only				
Cost of materials	$50	$50	$5,000	$5,000
Wage cost + labor burden	$445	$2,223	$445	$2,223
Overhead @ 114% (of labor only)	$507	$2,535	$507	$2,535
Break-even point	$1,002	$4,808	$5,952	$9,758

Effect	Difference	Difference	Difference	Difference
	+39%	**+45%**	**−25%**	**−7%**

Direct costs	=	$ 597,293	
Fixed costs	=	$ 187,484 = 31.4% of Direct costs	
Variable costs	=	$ 86,120 = 14.4% of Direct costs	
Total costs	=	**$870,897**	

FIGURE 6–6: **Comparison of Overhead Recovery Methods**

Regardless of the inconsistencies, we recommend testing these methods both internally and against the competition to determine if one of the methods is preferable to the other. In fact, different divisions within one company might use different methods. A key factor is to remain competitive with the other contractors in your area while making a reasonable profit.

Break-Even Point

The break-even point is the point at which you are now covering your expenses with income. It's important to know how much you will need in business to break even and recognize when you have reached that point. It often takes businesses a number of years before they show a profit; this is the turning point.

Refer to Figure 6–6 and study the data for Project A, Method A, numbers we will use for the remainder of this book, which indicates a break-even point of $722. This includes the wage costs and associated labor burden to complete the project as well as all the overhead related to these direct costs. As long as the costs stay within this budget, the company will begin to make a profit when they receive more than $722 for the project.

Budget Overview

Let's summarize the annual budget by combining the information gathered in Figures 6–2, 6–4, and 6–5. These include all of the anticipated costs of doing business during the entire year. In the next section, we break out the numbers and show how to prepare an estimate for an individual project. Following is the summary of the charts.

Fixed costs and variable costs are the components of overhead because they are the expenses that support the direct costs, the expenses directly related to the implementation of projects. As indicated earlier, total overhead in this case is 46 percent of direct costs. At this point, the level of total costs is useful only to give a general indication of how much revenue will be required to break even. However, this is true only at the level of direct costs indicated in Figure 6–2 (page 72). Chapter 7 covers the concept of contribution margin and the revenues required to generate a profit.

Preparing the Estimate

Preparing an estimate for an individual client can be a relatively easy task once an annual budget has been set and the cost of materials for the project determined. The only other major piece of information required is the amount of labor required to complete the project. The best way to do this is to make a chart of all the individual tasks your company does and assign a time budget for each. Each task should indicate the units involved (each, square feet, cubic yards, etc.) and the time required for a single employee to complete the task. Refer to Figure 6–7 for an example from a hypothetical landscape contracting company.

With this information in hand, you can begin to develop an estimate. We'll go through the process step by step using the following information. Upon completion, we'll use a spreadsheet to calculate a price for the job.

▶ Calculate average crew wage.
▶ Compile list of materials needed for the project.
▶ Refer to the time-per-task chart.
▶ Find the labor burden and overhead recovery percentages.
▶ Decide the desired profit.

Figure 6–8 on page 82 demonstrates a simple estimate using the spreadsheet:

▶ Column A is a list of the materials and tasks planned for the job.
▶ Column B indicates the unit associated with Column A.
▶ Column C shows the total quantity of each unit.
▶ Column D is the individual cost of each item.
▶ Column E is the total material cost achieved by multiplying column C by column D.
▶ Column F indicates the time it takes for one worker to complete one task; see Figure 6–7.

Time Required per Task

Task	Unit	Time
Prepare plant bed	square foot	0.25 hours
Plant 36" shrub	each	0.40 hours
Plant 2" shade trees	each	2.5 hours
Mulch plant beds	cubic yard	.75 hours
Stake trees	each	.30 hours
Install drain tile	linear foot	.50 hours
Spread topsoil	cubic yard	.35 hours
Sow grass seed	pound	.15 hours

FIGURE 6–7: **Sample Worksheet for Time Required Per Task**

Simple Estimate

	A	B	C	D	E	F	G	H
	Description	Unit	Quantity	Unit Cost of Material	Total Cost of Materials	Time per Task Notes	Total Time in Hours	Explanation
1	Prepare plant bed	sq. feet	200	$0	$0	0.03	5.00	
2	2" shade trees	each	2	$100	$200	2.50	5.00	
3	36" shrub	each	5	$35	$175	0.40	2.00	
4	Stake trees	each	2	$5	$10	0.30	0.60	
5	Mulch	cubic yard	3	$20	$60	0.75	2.25	
6	Spread topsoil	cubic yard	20	$20	$400	0.35	7.00	
7	Sow grass seed	pound	5	$4	$20	0.15	0.75	
8								
9	**Totals**				**$865**		**22.60**	
10								
11	Average crew wage						$22.21	
12	Cost of labor						$501.95	22.60 hours x $22.21
13	**Total direct cost**						**$1,366.95**	Materials plus labor
14	Overhead recovery %						46%	
15	Overhead cost						$628.80	$1366.95 x 0.46
16	**Break-even point**						**$1,995.75**	$1366.95 + $628.80

FIGURE 6-8: **Example of a Simple Estimate**

▶ Column G shows the total time to complete all tasks; Column F times Column C.

▶ Row 9 shows the totals of both the materials and the time required to complete the project.

▶ Row 11 indicates the average crew wage (see below).

▶ Row 12 indicates the total wage cost, including the labor burden calculated in Figure 6–1.

▶ Row 13 is the total direct cost for the project.

▶ Row 15 is the cost of overhead from page 75.

▶ Row 16 is the sum of Row 18 and Row 20, showing the break-even point of the project.

The average crew wage needs a bit more explanation. Step 1 is to add the wages of the individual workers expected to work on the project and divide by the number of workers; Step 2 adds the labor burden. The concept is to find an average crew wage because this ties in directly with the information from Figure 6–7. An average crew wage is the average paid to one worker while the time required per task is the amount of time required for one worker to complete the task. If K&K Contracting decides to place one two-person crew on the project, the wages of the two workers are $18.75 and $12.50:

Step 1:   ($18.75 + $12.50) ÷ 2 = $15.625 per hour = average crew wage

Step 2: $15.625 x labor burden percent from Figure 6–1
$15.625 x .421 = $6.58 = average labor burden per employee
$15.625 + $6.58 = $22.21 per hour = average crew wage

Therefore, we entered $22.21 in Row 11 of the spreadsheet and used the time per task information to calculate the total cost of labor for the project (Row 12).

The method used in this example is very beneficial because it can be used even if the number of workers on the project changes. Using the spreadsheet, it was determined that it will take one worker 22.60 actual hours to complete the project; with two workers the project should be completed in 11.30 actual hours. Should the owners decide to add another two-person work crew, they'd be free to do so without worrying about the effect on the bottom line.

Profits: The Bottom Line

"The worst crime against the working people is a company which [sic]
fails to operate at a profit."

—SAMUEL GOMPERS, WHO FOUNDED THE AMERICAN FEDERATION OF LABOR IN 1886

▶ Efficiency

Budgeting is one thing, but spending is another. For example, you may have budgeted $5,000 for advertising and marketing. The question is which is the most cost effective, efficient way in which to spend that money? Major corporations spend a great amount of time determining the most efficient ways of spending money. You want to find cost-efficient ways of purchasing items and paying for services, but you will also need to determine how these choices will or will not benefit your business. Like playing a game of chess, you need to consider the repercussions of each move before you make it. This makes the difference between efficiently and inefficiently run businesses.

Thus far we've discussed only the cost of doing business, without regard to revenues or profits. You've learned that there are costs that are directly related to the process of implementing a project; then there are overhead costs, some of which are related to the direct costs and others that will be incurred regardless of the amount of direct costs.

Profit is what you have left over after paying all of your expenses. If you were to study the income statement of a large corporation like the Walt Disney Company, you'd find columns and rows with data showing "gross profit," "operating income," "income before tax," "income after tax," "income before extraordinary items," and "net income." The discussion of these items is left to the accounting professors. The focus here is on net income.

However, net income is not the only measure of financial success. Investment advisors and specialists consider many factors when studying the financial statements of corporations. Again, it can be a very complex and time-consuming process to understand the profitability and success of a business. For our purposes here, we'll keep it simple. While every owner must determine what level of profit is acceptable, we'll use 12 percent as a profit goal when pricing services. Using this as a benchmark will allow for payment of year-end bonuses or dividends, upgrading buildings and equipment, and building up an emergency fund.

stat fact

According to industry sources, the average net income as a percentage of revenues within the contracting industry ranges from 3 to 5 percent. This means that a company with $1.2 million in revenues can expect to have a net income, after all expenses, of between $36,000 and $60,000.

▶ **Accounting 101**

Accountants, financial officers, and investors study financial statements in many different ways. I'll touch on three terms that sound similar but are quite different. While there are no "magic numbers," it may be an interesting and useful exercise to track these ratios on an annual basis. If the ratios increase, you can smile; if they decrease, don't frown—just work harder and more efficiently.

1. Return on equity equals net profit after taxes divided by stockholders' equity. It measures a company's efficiency at generating profits from dollars invested in the business. Return on equity is irrelevant if earnings are not reinvested in the company.

2. Return on assets equals net profit after taxes divided by total assets. It's an important gauge of profitability as it gives insight into the ability of management to generate profits from the assets available to the company.

3. Return on capital equals net income after taxes divided by long-term debt plus common stock. It is a measure of how effectively a company uses the money, both borrowed and owned, that is invested in the company.

The question is how to determine the price to charge and make a 12 percent profit. If you refer to Figure 6–8 on page 82, we see that the break-even point for the project is $1,996. Many people would venture a guess and say "to make a 12 percent profit, just multiply $1,996 by 12 percent and add the two numbers." Well, they are wrong. If you just read this sentence and shook your head, you are not alone. Now read the next sentence carefully and memorize it:

> To make a 12 percent profit on a project, divide the break-even point
> by one minus the desired profit (shown as a decimal).

Read it again. To make a 12 percent profit, you divide the break-even point by 0.88.

An example will make this seemingly crazy mathematical formula make sense. Suppose you sell a product for $100 and make a 10 percent profit; your break-even point is $100—$10, or $90. However, if you add 10 percent to $90, you get $99, $1 short of what you want. However, if you divide $90 by (1.00—.10), you arrive back at $100.

Now go back to Figure 6–8 with a break-even point of $1,996. To charge enough to make a 12 percent profit, you divide $1,996 by 0.88 and come up with a final cost of $2,268.

Wrap-Up

▶ Many new businesses fail because they fail to properly manage their finances.

▶ Establishing a financial budget is a key ingredient to business success.

▶ Computer spreadsheets are invaluable tools for establishing a budget.

▶ The true cost of labor includes payroll taxes, government-mandated insurance, employee benefits, and overtime.

▶ Overhead comprises fixed costs and variable costs.

▶ Pricing systems must be designed to recover overhead expenses.

▶ Three elements determine the final price to the consumer: direct labor and materials costs, overhead recovery, and profit.

▶ Profits are not made until revenues reach, and then surpass, the break-even point.

Contribution Margin and the Impact on Profits

For those of you who are still scratching your heads over the Accounting 101 sidebar in the last chapter, rest easy. You are not alone. The fact of the matter is that math scares lots of people, primarily because the language of math is so different from normal human communication. For fun, take the little quiz in Figure 7–1, the "Math Terms Worksheet" on page 88, to test your math prowess.

Math Terms Worksheet

Study the following ten math terms. Place a check mark next to the ones you understand or can define. (No cheating allowed!)

____ Algorithm

____ Exponential function

____ Divergence theorem

____ Permutations

____ Heaviside function

____ Differential equation

____ Distributive property

____ Transitive property

____ Scientific number

____ Sigma notation

FIGURE 7–1: **Math Worksheet**

*"Mathematics is made up of 50 percent formulas, 50 percent proofs,
and 50 percent imagination."*
—Unknown

How many were you able to check off? For those of you who know all ten terms, you are in the wrong field. Close the book and contact MIT immediately. But seriously, knowledge of higher math is not a requirement for success in business. Even those with limited exposure to algebra should be able to master the concepts of contribution margin presented in this chapter.

How to Calculate Contribution Margin

Contribution margin is a valuable mathematical tool that will help with your financial planning in two important ways. First, it will tell you how much revenue you must generate during the year in order to break even, and second, how much profit you will make on each dollar of revenue after reaching your break-even point. The major difficulty is initially estimating the amount of annual revenues your company expects to generate. Once again, we suggest communicating with industry associations, fellow contractors, and former employers to arrive at a reasonable revenue projection. Also look for websites and articles online such as Construction Business Owner (at www.constructionbusinessowner.com) to learn more about the financial side of your industry and how to make your business profitable.

Keep in mind that "profit," as used in this book, is unlike the actual taxable profit that a company reports on its state and federal income tax forms. Other factors, such as depreciation and prepaid expenses, have an effect on taxes due. In addition, the accounting method, cash or accrual, has significant effect on taxes. This is just another reason why it is critical to engage a qualified accountant to plan your year-end tax strategy and to prepare tax returns. Your accountant should also understand the big picture and not only focus on each year separately. Tax planning for one year can and will affect upcoming years, especially when making purchases or reviewing income patterns. Make sure your accountant is also thinking long term.

Contribution margin is defined as "the amount of revenue remaining after paying direct costs and variable costs that is available to pay fixed costs and profits." It is used as both a dollar amount and as a percentage.

The formula we will use for contribution margin is:

$$\text{Contribution margin (CM)} =$$
$$\text{Revenues} - (\text{Direct costs} + \text{Variable costs})$$

Using the example in Chapter 6 (Figures 6–2 and 6–5 on pages 72 and 77), taking a bit of artistic license and estimating annual revenues at $900,000, you arrive at the following contribution margin:

$$\text{CM} = \$900,000 - (\$597,293 + \$86,120)$$
$$\text{CM} = \$900,000 - \$683,413$$
$$\text{CM} = \$216,587$$

What this shows is that you have $216,587 available to pay for fixed costs, the expenses that do not change even when revenue changes, and profit.

A new formula calculates the contribution margin ratio:

$$\text{Contribution margin ratio (CMR)} = \text{Contribution margin} \div \text{revenues}$$
$$\text{CMR} = \$216,587 \div \$900,000$$
$$\text{CMR} = 0.2406 \text{ (or 24.06\%)}$$

For accuracy, we recommend carrying out the fraction to four decimal points. For you math cowards, we are nearly finished with formulas. If you read this chapter several times and work through the calculations yourself, it will become much clearer to you. You might even try the formulas with different estimated revenue figures to learn the effect on your budget.

The contribution margin ratio has two useful functions. First, you'll determine, based on fixed costs, at what point your revenue produces a break-even situation. The contribution margin ratio will probably change from year to year, and we recommend tracking the ratio and using a two- or three-year average when you set up your annual budget. Here's another useful formula:

Break-even point (BEP) = Fixed costs ÷ CMR
BEP = $187,588 ÷ 0.2406
BEP = $779,235

This means that if actual fixed costs meet the budget, the company will begin to generate a profit when revenues exceed $779,235. How much of a profit will be made is revealed by using the following (and final) formula:

Profit = (Revenue—Break-even revenue) x CMR
Profit = ($900,000—$779,235) x 0.2406
Profit = $120,765 x 0.2406
Profit = $29,056

Even though actual revenue exceeds break-even revenue by more than $119,000, the actual profit is far less because the difference was used for direct and variable costs spent generating the additional income.

For most contracting businesses, the ideal time to reach the break-even point is in early fall; doing so leaves several months to generate a profit. If the break-even point is reached in December, for example, the profit will likely be small. Study Figure 7–2 on page 91, and it should become clear.

Figure 7–2 shows how revenues and expenses grow during the year. Total costs, which include direct, fixed, and variable costs, are shown by the line with arrows. Revenues are shown by the line with tiny x marks. In the example, revenues begin to exceed costs during the month of August and remain ahead of costs for the remainder of the year, resulting in a profit for the company. Of course this is assuming a fairly steady work flow with similarly sized jobs throughout the year. You could have a major job, your largest of the year, in May and June, bringing you past your break-even point much earlier than expected. This can give you an opportunity to allow early profits to grow by year's end.

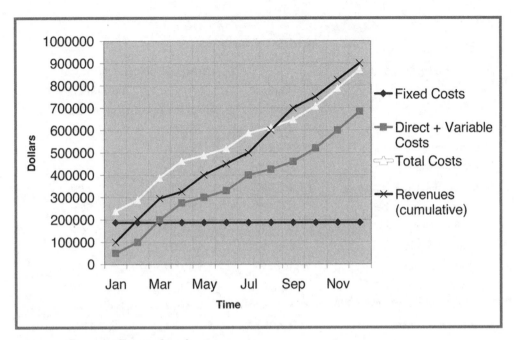

FIGURE 7-2: **Break-Even Analysis**

The Doctor Is In

Establishing a budget, understanding and using contribution margin, and correctly allocating expenses among direct, fixed, and variable costs are only the first steps in implementing a successful budget and estimating system. In order to be successful, expenses and revenues must be monitored on a regular basis and adjusted if necessary. The budget should be reviewed at least monthly for most small contracting businesses and at least quarterly for larger companies. A budget is not a static document but is subject to change and modification during the year. A change in the budget may necessitate a change in the way products and services are estimated, resulting in a price change. The sooner that a company can determine that expenses are not meeting budget expectations, the sooner pricing can be adjusted to reflect the discrepancies.

Figure 7–3 on page 92 is an example of monitoring spending on a monthly basis. Spending through September is compared with the 12-month budget. Column 2 lists the amounts, by category, that are budgeted for the entire year; column 3 lists the amounts actually spent as of September 30; column 4 indicates the percentage of the annual budget that has been spent. Because September represents 75 percent of the year, the expectation is

Budget Analysis

Direct Cost Budget	Spent through 9/30/xx		
	Annual Expense	75% of the Year	Percent of Total Budget Spent
ABC Contractors Supply	$85,000	$65,000	76%
Continental Materials	$110,000	$80,000	73%
USA Hardware	$35,000	$32,000	91%
County Builders & Supply	$55,000	$42,500	77%
Jones & Jones Lumber	$30,000	$24,000	80%
All-State-Rent-It-All	$17,500	$10,000	57%
National Plastics	$25,000	$15,000	60%
Foreman's wages	$101,250	$80,000	79%
Laborers' wages	$67,500	$52,000	77%
Labor burden @ 42.1%	$71,043	$55,572	78%
Total direct costs	**$597,293**	**$456,072**	**76%**
Fixed-Cost Budget			
Kate's salary	$40,000	$30,000	75%
Ken's salary	$40,000	$30,000	75%
Office assistant salary	$24,000	$18,000	75%
Labor burden @ 19.6%	$20,384	$15,288	75%
Insurance (building/vehicle)	$3,000	$2,300	77%
Health insurance (office staff)	$10,000	$7,500	75%
Telephone	$900	$700	78%
Cellular phones (5)	$3,000	$2,500	83%
Yellow pages advertising	$1,200	$900	75%
Bank payments	$25,000	$18,750	75%
Capital equipment fund	$5,000	$3,750	75%
Licenses	$1,200	$900	75%
Utilities	$1,800	$1,550	86%
Rent	$12,000	$9,000	75%
Total Fixed Costs	$186,484	$141,138	75%

FIGURE 7–3: **Budget Analysis**

Get a checkup using a spreadsheet set up like this to compare your budget to actual expenses.

Budget Analysis

Direct Cost Budget	Spent through 9/30/xx		
	Annual Expense	75% of the Year	Percent of Total Budget Spent
Fixed-Cost Budget			
% of Direct Costs	31%	31%	
Variable-Cost Budget			
Miscellaneous expenses	$6,000	$4,000	67%
Gasoline/diesel fuel	$15,000	$13,000	87%
Advertising	$5,000	$4,000	80%
Postage	$750	$500	67%
Printing	$1,000	$500	50%
Office supplies	$4,000	$3,000	75%
Hardware store/small tools	$3,000	$2,450	82%
Equipment repairs	$10,000	$4,000	40%
Uniforms	$900	$900	100%
Employee yard time	$18,750	$13,500	72%
Employee incentives & bonuses	$6,000	$3,500	58%
Labor burden @ 42.1%	$10,419	$7,157	69%
Cell phones (portion)	$300	$250	83%
Contingency	$2,000	$100	5%
Returns	$3,000	$2,000	67%
Total Variable Costs	$86,120	$58,857	68%
% of Direct Costs	14%	13%	

FIGURE 7–3: **Budget Analysis,** continued

that most expense categories be close to this figure. Amounts that are far over or far under the budget should be analyzed further.

While several items are over budget, the totals for each category are acceptable; total direct costs are 76 percent of budget, fixed costs are right on budget at 75 percent, and variable costs are under budget at 68 percent. Two items are worth considering in more detail. Utilities have an annual budget of $1,800, but $1,550, or 86 percent of budget has been spent. An analysis may show that seasonal temperatures caused utility expenses to rise earlier in the year, but they are expected to drop in later months. The uniforms expenses are at 100 percent of budget. Here, an analysis may indicate that new uniforms were purchased in January. No more uniforms will be purchased before the end of the year, so the annual expense will meet the budget. In the example of Figure 7–3, it appears that total spending is very close to the budget, and there is no need to adjust the pricing formula.

A second method of tracking the success or failure of company operations has little to do with the budget or with contribution margin. However, it is a useful tool, especially when used over the course of several years. This method compares actual revenues with real field labor costs, which are regular wages plus overtime costs. It is unnecessary to add labor burden to the calculations. Wages of office staff, sales staff, and executives are not included as they are not direct job costs. Consider Figure 7–4.

As shown, at the end of September 2013, revenues were $580,000 and total wages were $127,500. Therefore, each dollar spent on field wages generated $4.55 of revenue. In 2014, the amount generated dropped to $4.45, but it rebounded in 2012 to $4.59. For some reason, efficiency dropped in 2014; there could be any number of reasons for this drop, and they aren't necessarily all bad. It may be that the workforce did work less efficiently and took longer than expected to complete projects. It may also be just a quirk in the calendar—perhaps there was an extra pay period in 2014 or, possibly, several projects were near completion at the end of the month and their revenues are not factored into the equation. But whenever there is a drop in efficiency as indicated by a reduction in sales-per-labor dollar, it is necessary to learn why the drop occurred. Any drop in efficiency is a red flag that may indicate a breakdown somewhere in the company. Perhaps the estimating department did not realize that there was a price increase in materials, or new employees are taking too long to learn their tasks, or the

Sales per Labor Dollar

Year	Month	Revenues	Regular Wages	Overtime	Total Wages	Sales per Labor Dollar
2013	September	$580,000	$117,500	$10,000	$127,500	$4.55
2014	September	$625,000	$129,000	$11,500	$140,500	$4.45
2015	September	$675,000	$135,000	$12,000	$147,000	$4.59

FIGURE 7–4: **Sample Spreadsheet to Analyze Sales per Labor Dollar**

billing department is tardy in sending invoices for work completed. Whatever the reason, it must be corrected immediately.

Tracking expenditures and revenues on a monthly basis and comparing them to the annual budget and to previous years' spending is a fairly simple task that should be done on a monthly basis, shortly after the end of each month. Routine financial check-ups will usually prevent serious problems that can have a negative impact on a company's bottom line.

Wrap-Up

▶ Contribution margin is the amount of revenue necessary to break even after paying direct, variable, and fixed costs.

▶ Contribution margin is used to calculate at what point during the year revenues produce a break-even situation.

▶ Contribution margin is used to determine how much profit is made from each dollar of revenue after the break-even point is reached.

▶ Small businesses should schedule a monthly "physical exam" to ensure that spending is in line with expectations.

Promoting Your Services

Company logos come in all sizes, shapes, and colors. A few, like the Nike swoosh and McDonald's golden arches, are so recognizable that the companies don't need to include their name with the logo. Many professional sports team simply have the swoosh sewn onto their uniforms; viewers instantly identify the logo with Nike. Children riding in the back seat of their parent's car do not need to be told that a McDonald's is just past the next intersection; the golden arches (although less prominent in recent years) announce the fact well in advance. These companies have spent millions of dollars establishing worldwide images that are directly linked to their logos.

> *"If you don't do it excellently, don't do it at all. Because if it's not excellent, it won't be profitable or fun, and if you're not in business for fun or profit, what the hell are you doing there?"*
> —ROBERT TOWNSEND

Unfortunately, small contracting companies do not have the resources to develop and promote such a recognizable logo. However, this fact should not prevent them from presenting a positive image to the public.

The term "marketing" has quite a few definitions, which vary widely depending upon the type of product or service being sold. The marketing strategy for a company selling toothpaste to consumers is much different than that of a company selling steel to automobile companies. However, simply put, "marketing" is any activity that connects producers with consumers. Marketers use knowledge of economics, psychology, sociology, anthropology, and strategy to project a positive image that increases demand for their products. Most contracting companies concentrate their marketing activities on customer needs, rather than product innovation, which is typical of a service business. They ask, "What do our customers need and how can we efficiently and profitably meet these needs?"

While many aspects of marketing may sound complicated and expensive, there are things that a new contracting company can do to promote itself to prospective customers without employing an expensive public relations company.

Get Your Website Up Immediately

The first place most people go to look for products and services providers is the internet. Everyone will want to know where to find you online, which means, like most new businesses today, you will want to have your website posted before even opening for business. Worst case scenario, you don't go into business and simply take the site down.

fun fact ☺

Nike developed its swoosh logo in the early 1970s. Company founder Phil Knight was facing a deadline and needed a logo. He paid the handsome sum of $35 for the swoosh design, commenting that he didn't love it. He eventually gave the designer stock in the company. I bet he really loves the logo today.

Designing a simple site is not difficult, and as your business grows, so can your website. Before designing a site, or asking someone to design one for you, a new business owner should look at the sites of service businesses to get an idea of the look that he or she wants for the website. While you cannot take someone else's content, you can certainly get the general idea of the layout and perhaps even colors that you want.

Sites should be fairly simple in the early stages since you are new and the lack of familiarity will send customers elsewhere if the site is slow to load or overly cluttered.

Typically your website will contain the following:

▶ *Homepage.* Photos of your work, a listing of what you offer, areas you serve, and a paragraph on why people want to work with you. Easy links to the other pages on your site (such as your About Us pages), and any relevant company current news is typically found on the homepage. Like the rest of the site, the homepage should take on the colors and concept used elsewhere for your business (such as on business cards, brochures, or anything else you use to promote yourself). You should also include a link to your Facebook page (which is also advised these days) and anywhere else you can be located. For an excellent example from a general contractor's website, visit the Sherri Builders' homepage at http://sherribuilders.com.

▶ *About Us.* Tell your story in a brief and clever way. Read other About Us pages to get an idea of what to say and then in your own words tell the story of how you got started and why. People don't need your life story, so edit, edit, edit. Keep it to a couple of paragraphs and a photo of yourself and perhaps your team. Don't be scared to open up a little bit by personalizing the page. We're living in an age in which people like knowing a little about the people with whom they are doing business.

▶ *Gallery.* Some pictures of jobs you have completed (with the consent of your clients). Update if you have recent jobs to add.

▶ *Press.* If anyone has written about you or your business, post, or link to, the story or blog. Hint:

tip

Don't forget, your website is up there day after day. Update it often. Keep it current. Provide fresh content such as recent jobs you've completed and any new services or special deals you are offering. Also, be informative and entertaining. For example, provide some handy home maintenance tips that your customers can do for themselves, not to replace your services, of course. If you can do so in an entertaining manner, people will keep coming back to your website often.

save the story on your computer in case the newspaper or magazine goes belly up and the link is no longer viable.

► *Contact Page.* Make sure people can reach you easily. Have your phone number and email available on every page.

You can also try to maximize your responses by offering online deals, such as 10 percent off if you respond via email by a certain date. Your goal is to start a dialogue about what contracting needs a client may have and how you can fulfill them in a cost effective way (without underselling yourself).

Once people respond to your website, make a smooth and early transition from emails to a phone call and even an in-person meeting to show them what you can do for them. Of course, you also need to make it clear, on the website, exactly where you do business. If you're based in Ann Arbor, Michigan, for example, someone from Boise, Idaho, probably won't be in your area.

Also, don't quote prices on your website, although you can give a range.

Web Layout and Design

Always put the most important data and great photos high up on the pages so that people need not scroll down and down. Also make sure your colors and graphics look good, not only on your computer screen but also on various mobile devices since more and more people are using their cell phones and tablets instead of their laptops. Don't waste time on fancy graphics that take too long to load. Nobody has time to wait.

There are plenty of web builder sites that will help you build it yourself such as http://web.com, www.wix.com, www.weebly.com, www.godaddy.com, and https://wordpress.com, among others. A couple of sites you might visit that specialize in contractor websites include http://contractorgorilla.com and www.contractorweb.net, or you can hire a web designer. Look for recommendations from other business owners you know. Once you find someone, look at their portfolio of website designs

If you look for a local web designer in your area, make sure to show her other sites that you like, and be sure that she develops a site that is user-friendly and easy to maneuver. It's your business, so get what you want. Remember, as a service provider your site is a business card of sorts to get them to email or call you; that means you do not need retail features like a shopping cart. Don't spend money on unnecessary features.

From a technical standpoint, it is important that all pages link easily to the information the individual is seeking. Don't make visitors to your website jump hurdles to find what they are looking for or they will give up. Check links often to make sure they are still working. Also, you want to try to build a contact list using your website. If you give something away, they may be more than happy to provide their email address so you can reach out to them. Such a giveaway can be anything from a 5 percent discount to the first ten people who book you for a job to a free download of interest to your audience.

warning

Look carefully at the other sites a web designer has done in the past before hiring someone. If they all appear to have a similar style and it's not what you want, do not assume for a second that this person can deviate from the norm just for you. Habits are hard to break. You need someone who sees your vision, not a variation of her own.

Establishing an Online Presence

As many business owners have learned over the past decade, just because you have a website doesn't mean people will find it. Even if you optimize your site with keywords, links, and other tricks of the trade, that still doesn't assure you that people will flock to it. You need to draw people to your website. One way to do so is to build your presence on social media through a Facebook page, Twitter posts, and photos on sites like Instagram, Pinterest, and Tumblr.

Linking with other retailers and getting your listing in all local online directories also draws attention to your website. You will also want to get yourself on Angie's List (at https://www.angieslist.com) which can be a godsend to contractors, particularly with local listings that can be read by your potential clients. Of course you need to get positive reviews. The same goes for Yelp (www.yelp.com).

As for your own social media postings, you want to show your expertise in conversations and by helping people who are seeking solutions. Social media is for letting people get to know you, NOT for hard selling. Think of yourself at a party. Would you approach possible customers with a sales pitch or with a polite conversation that touches upon the needs of the person to whom you are talking? Then, if you can work what you do into the conversation more generically, you can let them know what you do.

You can also draw in new business by adding tidbits of clever information, trivia, e-cards, jokes, or anything else relating to the type of contracting your business does. Then spread the word, share with friends or fans, re-tweet comments on Twitter, or post a video on YouTube, but first make sure it's NOT boring. Then share it by linking to it from your site and through word of mouth. Be creative and generate a buzz. If you can "go viral" to any extent that means those who see it spread the word for you—it's free promotion! This way your followers and clients help promote your business. Perhaps you create something humorous on how NOT to build, and then show them the correct way in which you could build. Keep it simple, fun, and concise—and make sure your contact info is easy to read.

Self-Promotion

One successful trick of the trade is to promote your company through the use of free coverage in local newspapers, magazines, in blogs, and on other websites. Many newspapers have a Sunday home improvement section that offers tips and suggestions for home remodeling and landscaping. The editors of these sections are constantly looking for the local expert to assist in the development of articles. A contractor who is mentioned in the article or offers money-saving tips will gain instant credibility as an expert and reach many potential new customers at the same time. One landscaping company in the Midwest volunteered its employees to help eradicate invasive weeds at a local county park. The result was a front page article with several photographs showing the employees spraying the weeds with an herbicide. The only cost to the company was several hours of labor and a bit of chemicals; the goodwill and positive image projected by the company was invaluable. In the eyes of many consumers, this company became the local expert for control of invasive weeds. One of the goals of such an endeavor is to let the community know what the company does in a positive and constructive way. Becoming the local expert who sees a problem and offers a solution will pay dividends well beyond the cost of time spent preparing for the event.

Another approach to marketing and public relations is to offer free services to the community. Local nonprofit organizations hold fundraising events during the year and are constantly looking for items for an auction or a raffle. Contractors with design services can offer their services to help these organizations raise money. Others may donate coupons that offer savings on either products or services. Here again, the cost to the contractor is relatively small and the goodwill very large.

New companies can issue press releases to their local newspapers informing the public of these charitable endeavors. However, press releases can go further as well

tip

Look for blogs that include interviews or guest bloggers. While the internet will reach a much broader audience than you need, it will also blanket your community with your expertise, since nearly everyone gets the web without having to go out and buy a newspaper or magazine.

by announcing what's new at the company—be it new employees, employee promotions, new products and services, or company milestones.

Demographics

For any type of marketing you plan to do, it is essential that you know your customer demographics and the demographics of any media in which you decide to advertise or write articles or blogs. What age range and income bracket is most receptive to your marketing? When posting online or buying ads in magazines or newspapers, what is the circulation and to what age group and income level? Demographics let you know if you are reaching the people who need and could afford your services.

It's advantageous to get an idea of what other success-ful contractors have been doing on social media over the past few years. You can learn from those who have been there and done that. See where they post and what type of information they provide about their areas of specialty and for their customers.

You also want to pay attention to the responses you are getting, not only on social media but at review sites like Yelp (www.yelp.com) and Angie's List (www.angieslist.com). What do people like or dislike about what you are doing? What postings are generating likes? You can learn a lot from your followers and customers. Keep in mind that just as quickly as social media can help you, you may take a negative turn if you get into arguments with those who've posted bad reviews, and this can hurt your reputation.

If you get legitimate bad press (based on something that went wrong) you need to be honest, humble, forthright, and apologetic. In short, be ready to put out fires and make amends when necessary.

save

Advertising in the telephone directory can be very expensive for a new business. One way to save money is to list your company's website address in the directory rather than purchase a display ad. While the future of the printed version of the Yellow Pages is bleak, internet editions are a very important means of promoting yourself. Look for local directories.

Print It!

While the internet is an incredible tool for business, many elderly citizens are not computer savvy and do not use a computer. Many others use the computer and internet for shopping and information, but not to shop for contracting services. For these folks, print advertising is still a valuable tool. Costs vary depending on the type of print media used.

▶ What's in a Name?

The name you choose for your business should reflect your market niche, identify you and your services, and be easy to say and spell. For example, Habibullaev & Associates is difficult to say and means nothing; on the other hand, Barefoot Lawn Care, one of our favorites, gets its message across immediately and positively. Likewise, Paula's Petals makes good sense for a florist, but can anyone imagine what Pete's Photosynthetic Management Group LLC does? Also, make sure your company name can be used on your website—do a search for the domain name that best suits your business name. They should be the same with a .com at the end, or .net if .com is taken. So if your business is Kramer Contracting, you want to be able to use KramerContracting.com, or .net. Search for domain names even before choosing your company name.

A simple approach is to prepare fliers that can be dropped off at individual homes. Some contractors who deliver colorful and informative fliers to all the homes in the neighborhood where they are currently working.

Advertising in major metropolitan newspapers can become very expensive; local community newspapers offer better values, especially for new contractors who wish to limit their services to a small geographical area. These papers periodically print special sections that appeal to home improvement shoppers.

Because magazine readership is significantly down, you may look to post ads in small local circulars or fliers instead. Local community-based websites can often give you a good rate for frequent advertising. Advertising is more significant when seen often, and these smaller, but very localized, publications allow you to get more bang (placements) for your buck. Other options for adverting and promotion include:

- ▶ *Mailings.* Typically something like a postcard or a flier can work but be careful; often you do not get enough response to make the process of making something to send—printing it, getting a mailing list together, and taking the time to send it—cost effective.
- ▶ *Placemats or menus at local diners or pizza places.* This can be an inexpensive yet effective method. It is estimated by the Entrepreneur Business Idea Center that a 50 seat restaurant uses about 6,000 placemats a month.
- ▶ *Your local Little League team.* Sponsoring a team is great way to introduce yourself to the community

▶ *Local bulletin boards.* Put up a flier at the library, post office, at some restaurants, etc.

Word of Mouth

By far the best, most successful, and cheapest form of marketing your company is "word of mouth." A happy client is much more likely to tell his or her friends and neighbors about the great work you've done for him than one who merely thought you did an average job. An unhappy client can do more harm to your business than nearly anything else.

Recently, a small contractor surveyed its clients and asked them which medium they were most likely to use when shopping for contracting services. "Word of mouth" was the winner. While small businesses usually cannot carry out in-depth marketing studies, the more they know about their clients, the more chances they'll have of increasing sales. Knowing your clients' typical age, approximate income level, and personal preferences allows you to tailor your products and services to meet their particular needs. As mentioned earlier, learn about your customer demographics.

Several techniques can be used to increase the chances that a client will give your company a good recommendation. Chapter 10 discusses relationships with clients in more detail, but from a marketing aspect the following are critical to creating and maintaining an excellent reputation:

▶ *Communicate with the client.* All clients appreciate knowing that their project is the most important one you are working on. Also leave them your business card (with your phone number and your website and email address on it).

▶ *Present a professional image.* Employees in the field should look and dress like professionals. The best way to achieve this is to require that employees wear clean uniforms while on the job. The uniforms do not have to be fancy or expensive. T-shirts with

▶ Sign Up

There are a lot of associations and organizations covering all types of contractors. If you search online for associations for contractors you'll find government, independent, roofing, electrical, drilling, and many more associations. Some are quite large, such as the Associated Builders and Contractors of America (at www.ABC.org), with over 20,000 chapter members. Membership in associations enhances your credibility, plus they can help you get answers to questions in your industry and provide guidance on legal or financial issues.

your company logo are usually acceptable, but they must be clean and well maintained. Smoking while on the job should be limited to breaks. (If you can get away with it, we suggest prohibiting all smoking during the workday.) Finally, vehicles should be well maintained, clean, and the same color. Remember the fraudulent asphalt sealers in the Preface? Their van was rusty and had no name or logo on the side; most likely it spewed black, smelly exhaust as they drove off with poor Mr. Jones's money.

▶ *Train employees, and discuss with subcontractors the importance of showing respect to your clients.* It's important that whoever is working on your behalf understand that you don't really pay their wages—the client does. While working at the job site, your employees should be able to answer basic questions posed by the client. If they do not know the answer to a question, they must tell the client that they don't know but will either find the answer or refer it to someone in the company who can answer it. Typically they should be able to text or call you, or someone else in the company, to get the answers. Clients appreciate both diligence and honesty; your employees must have both. Your reputation is on the line.

▶ *Enter (and win) awards competitions.* Many contracting business associations have annual competitions that allow members to display their best work; the best are often recognized at an awards banquet. Preparing for an awards competition can be time-consuming and expensive, but shortcuts cannot be taken when preparing an entry. These competitions are usually judged by a panel of your industry peers who know a substandard job when they see it. The publicity that results from winning an award is priceless because clients love doing business with companies that are among the best in their field.

Too Much of a Good Thing?

While everyone strives for success, too much of a good thing can occasionally lead to problems that overwhelm a business. Each business should strive for a professional and successful marketing and public relations campaign; but each business must also be able to meet the demands that might be generated from successful advertising. Some businesses find themselves in a situation where they are growing faster than their ability to provide quality and timely service. Anticipation of growth before it occurs will help prevent potential bottlenecks in providing goods and services to your clients. In particular, rapidly growing companies often find themselves in trouble in some or all of the following areas:

▶ *Lack of skilled foremen and workers.* This weakness makes it difficult to complete projects with the expected high quality.

▶ *Scheduling conflicts.* Most clients do not want to wait eight or ten weeks for the commencement of their project, but some fast-growing contractors make unrealistic promises for project start dates.

▶ *Shortage of tools and equipment needed to complete the project.* This situation often results in the purchase of equipment beyond the amount budgeted or the need to rent expensive equipment on a short-term basis.

▶ *Cash flow.* Can the business keep up with expenditures? Increased business usually requires an increase in outlays for materials and labor, so the company must improve efforts to collect funds from clients.

A contracting company must understand these potential pitfalls and make contingency plans in the event that business activity grows "too fast." Rapid growth does not always follow successful marketing campaigns, but the company that fails to plan for it may become a statistic on the "business failures" list. There was a television commercial running that showed a group of employees press the button that launched their website. Then within moments, they got flooded with responses. At first they were thrilled, but then their initial smiles of success turned into worried expressions as they wondered what they would do to accommodate all the clients they received. In the real world, many businesses that signed up on Groupon, and other discount sites, got more customers than they could handle and found themselves in all sorts of water—in some instances they even ran themselves out of business. So, before you spread the word far and wide, make sure you have enough employees and/or subcontractors to handle the potential workload.

Wrap-Up

▶ Marketing is any activity that connects producers with consumers.

▶ Self-promotion is an excellent and inexpensive way to advertise your business.

▶ You should have your website designed and posted before you open your company.

▶ Word of mouth is the number-one way most contracting companies find new clients.

▶ Understanding the potential pitfalls of extremely rapid growth makes good business sense.

▶ The use of social media can be a great way of attracting new customers as well as maintaining good communications with existing clients.

▶ Make sure you can accommodate the workload that you may receive from advertising and marketing your services.

Get
a Job

As a contracting business grows, it is necessary to hire employees to assist in the many tasks of operating the business. Managing employees is one of the most difficult tasks any business owner faces. Contracting companies often face additional challenges because some sectors of the industry are seasonal and some specialties have a higher turnover rate than average.

"It's not what you pay a man, but what he costs you that counts."
—HUMORIST WILL ROGERS

Hiring and managing employees is a time-consuming task that is part psychology, part economics, and part organization. Attention to detail is required, not only for government and insurance reporting but also because employees will descend on the payroll department if they think there is even a small error in their paycheck or if it's delayed.

In spite of the headaches, hiring employees can be an extremely positive experience. Not only do they help the business grow and prosper, each employee also makes contributions to the personality of the company. When interviewing prospective employees, keep in mind the effect he or she will have on the mood and temperament of you, your business, and other employees.

The Employee Handbook

An employee handbook is a great tool for both employer and employee. As a company grows, it needs to create an employee handbook to document the employer's expectations of employees. The handbook will describe expected performance, how an employee can earn a raise or promotion, what fringe benefits are available, and other information such as work hours, dress code, and acceptable/unacceptable behavior. Owners can become better managers by participating in the process of creating the handbook because it will help them decide which policies are most important and most practical for their company. By setting guidelines and laying out some ground rules, a handbook can be a positive tool for improving morale and communications.

Both books and internet websites provide information about creating a handbook. In addition, it is usually wise to have your lawyer take a look at the document to ensure that you are not violating state or federal law.

Most contractor handbooks include at least the following items:

- ► Overview of your company
- ► Equal opportunity statement indicating that your hiring policies are nondiscriminatory
- ► Hours of work, lunch, and other breaks
- ► Wages and benefits, vacation and holiday pay
- ► Retirement plan rules and eligibility
- ► Safety policies and requirements
- ► Dress code
- ► Employment-at-will statement that says that employment can be terminated by the employer at any time for any reason

- Standards of conduct, policy on sexual harassment, smoking, alcohol use, disciplinary procedures
- Drug-testing policies
- Statement that the handbook is not a contract and that policies can be changed at any time
- Signature line for employees to acknowledge that they have read and understand the handbook

The handbook can be emailed to each employee with a date by which time employees should sign off on having read it. Hard copies should also be available. Hint: Try not to make it read as legalese or people are likely to forget what they've read or simply gloss over it. Make your points in an easy to follow manner… make your handbook concise and readable.

Applications and Hiring Forms

Job applications should be straightforward and easy for the prospective employee to complete. In addition to basic contact information, the application should ask for driver's license number, level of education, and special skills and have space to list several business references.

It is illegal to ask questions about race, gender, and age because these might lead to discrimination questions. Some states require that applicants fill out a special form that allows the employer to obtain detailed information about the applicant's motor vehicle record. A simple telephone call to verify references is essential. Some states provide public court records on the internet where employers can learn if an applicant has a criminal record.

Once hired, new employees must fill out Form I-9, "Employment Eligibility Verification," which proves that he or she is legally permitted to work in the United States, and Form W-4, which provides the employee's Social Security number and indicates the allowances (deductions) she or he is claiming for income tax purposes.

Job Descriptions

Employers are also encouraged to develop written job descriptions for each job category in the company. These descriptions are useful not only to inform applicants about the job they are applying for but can also be used during the periodic employee review. Small businesses should conduct a review with each employee at least once per year to discuss overall performance and strategies for improvement. Employers should also seek suggestions about how to improve the way the company operates.

Written job descriptions must be more than a simple list of tasks to be performed; they should be results oriented by including desired outcomes of the job. The description should start with a job purpose, which is a general summary of the job, and then include the essential functions of the job. These summarize what the employee does to complete his or her specific tasks and includes sections related to the results of these tasks. Following are several examples of items that may be included in the results-oriented portion of the job description:

▶ Keeps equipment operating by following operating instructions; troubleshoots breakdowns; maintains supplies; performs preventative maintenance; schedules repairs

▶ Maintains a safe and secure workplace by adhering to company standards and policies and to legal regulations

▶ Contributes to company success by being respectful of clients and by helping other employees accomplish their tasks

Minors Are Major

A major concern of many contracting companies is the hiring of minor employees, those under 18 years of age. Most states require that minor employees obtain a work permit prior to beginning a job. Depending upon their age, minors may be prevented from operating most power tools, driving company-owned vehicles, and assisting in "dangerous" work. The federal government has issued regulations covering the maximum hours a minor may work, both by the day and by the week. The United States Department of Labor has links to more detailed information on its website, which can be found at www.dol.gov.

Wages and Benefits

Many owners of contracting businesses will, when asked, tell you that, "I probably work for about fifty cents an hour." While untrue, it sometime feels like it. On the other hand, most employees choose a job because they think that they will like the work and they are satisfied with the salary. A positive workplace with caring bosses does a lot to create a successful work environment, but competitive wages and benefits are what maintain the success.

Most segments of the contracting industry are unique in that the workplace changes from day to day or week to week. Workers who choose to work for contractors enjoy the variety of jobs they perform as well as the prospect of working outdoors and/or working at different locations. While some factory jobs may offer higher wages, the typical successful contracting employee would go crazy with the daily routine often found in a factory.

Many industry associations conduct periodic wage and benefit surveys and share the results with the participating companies. Contractors that take advantage of this opportunity can become more competitive because they know what their competitors are paying on average for wages and benefits; knowledge of typical wages and benefits is also useful because employers can prove to their own employees that they are keeping pace with the industry.

While benefits may be seen as the icing on the cake, most employees expect them. Employers who fail to offer these benefits will likely suffer higher turnover and have a less skilled and dedicated work force. Typically, however, most employers institute a probationary period of several months before an employee is eligible for benefits. It makes little sense to give a new employee a paid day off after working for only a few weeks.

- ▶ Paid holidays are expected by all employees. Typically six holidays are covered as legal holidays, but some employers include the day after Thanksgiving as a working day.

- ▶ Paid vacations, based on years of service, are another expected benefit. Seasonal contractors may wish to take into account the fact that many of their employees may be on layoff for several months.

- ▶ Retirement plans, while not yet universal, are becoming more popular each year, but most are predicated on the employee contributions. The problems faced by our Social Security system, coupled with the demise of corporate pension plans, make it more imperative than ever that all workers take steps to prepare for their own retirement. Larger companies can offer a 401(k) plan, giving their employees the opportunity to invest pre-tax wages that will grow tax free; the employer may make contributions to employees' accounts as well. The Roth 401(k) has contributors paying taxes up-front to make tax-free withdrawals during retirement. It has certain advantages over the traditional IRA, but all tax considerations need to be taken into considerations. These plans may be expensive and somewhat complicated to administer. Small contractors have another option called the "SIMPLE IRA." As the name implies, this plan is much easier to administer and is inexpensive for the employer. Unlike the 401(k), however, employers must make either matching or non-elective contributions to each employee's account.

- ▶ Use of a company vehicle, if offered, requires tedious record-keeping, especially if the employee uses the vehicle for personal use. The value of the personal use must be included in the employee's taxable income. The rules and regulations established by the federal government are very complicated. The decision to offer this benefit should be made only after consultation with your lawyer and accountant.

▶ Raises are not actually a benefit, but employers should have a policy in place regarding wage and salary raises. Most contractors give raises once per year, after the annual employee review and when merited during the year on a case-by-case basis. Any employee promoted to a more responsible position should receive a raise, as should newer employees whose progress is above and beyond expectations. While most employers do not share wage rates among employees, employees certainly know what others make. Employers should provide at the minimum, an annual cost of living raise. No raises, or those that do not keep up with inflation, will typically lead to low morale and high turnover, which means training new people. In the end, turnover and additional training will typically cost more than giving employees at least a cost-of-living increase.

tip

Employees who violate company rules or policies should receive a written warning explaining the error and what will happen to the employee if the error is repeated. By maintaining a written paper trail of policy violations, an employer both protects himself from future legal action initiated by a disgruntled employee and gives the employer ammunition when a troublesome employee demands a pay raise.

▶ Incentive plans offer an employer a creative way to reward productive and successful employees. While bonuses paid annually based on increases in sales or profits are a fine way to reward employees, it can be more valuable to give the bonus closer to the time when it was earned. Some companies reward employees immediately after a successful project is completed or pay out bonuses on a monthly basis. The most successful incentive plans reward individual effort on a continuing basis as well as companywide success on an annual basis. For new companies that are not yet able to provide bonuses, non-financial rewards, such as an additional vacation day or even an award/public acknowledgment, can be considered. Be creative— know what your people would appreciate.

▶ Helping employees pay for continuing education can reap rewards for employers. Technical colleges offer courses that improve employees' abilities and do not conflict with the workday. Some associations offer certification classes where employees can learn more about their jobs and their industry. In both of these cases, the employer can assist with tuition and fees. By advertising and sharing the accomplishments of their employees, contracting businesses can both honor their employees and attract a more affluent clientele.

Turnover

"A good manager doesn't try to eliminate conflict; he tries to keep it from wasting the energies of his people. If you're the boss and your people fight you openly when they think that you are wrong—that's healthy."
—Robert Townsend

Many companies in the contracting industry are victims of higher-than-average rates of employee turnover. Training new employees is a time-consuming and expensive undertaking, so it makes good business sense to try to hold onto your best employees. Providing a competitive wage and benefit package helps reduce turnover, but is not the only way to retain employees. Another factor that rates very highly with laborers is an enjoyable work environment where employees feel that they are part of a team and are respected and appreciated by their bosses as well as peers. Bosses who have an open-door policy that gives all employees the opportunity to speak personally with the owners of the company are usually more respected than authoritarian bosses who intimidate their employees. Happy employees who work under a competitive compensation package are much more productive than employees who are constantly grumbling about the poor working conditions they are forced to work under.

An often-overlooked managerial technique is simply listening to employees. New ideas often come from subordinates because they are the ones actually

save

Workers' compensation rates for contracting companies are typically very high due to the risks associated with the tasks performed. While the rates are established by a government-controlled bureau, the insurance companies that provide coverage offer a variety of incentive plans in which companies with good safety records receive part of their premiums back. As these rebates can be upwards of 50 percent of the total premium for large companies, an excellent incentive to promote safety is to share a portion of the rebate with safe employees. By implementing a safety contest that rewards safe employees, an employer can reduce the number of claims, which will ultimately result in high rebates. However, it should be noted that employees cannot be penalized for injuries and are required by law to report them to the employer.

▶ Payroll Decisions

As a company grows, it is more likely to employ an outside payroll service. But it's still a call you'll want to make—consider the pros and cons.

The benefits of outsourcing payroll include saving time; having skilled professionals with greater understanding of new payroll laws; and saving money in the long-term rather than paying people in house to do the job.

The benefits of in-house payroll include faster access to the data and saving money within a small company.

performing the tasks of the business. Owners and managers who encourage employees to make suggestions to improve the company help to create an atmosphere where employees feel both needed and important. Not only can a company benefit financially from new ideas, but the costs of turnover can be reduced because employees feel happy that they are contributing to success.

Organizational Chart

Creating an informal organizational chart will improve communication and, in turn, the efficiency of your office. Productivity increases when each department within a company understands not only its own responsibilities but also the duties and responsibilities of other departments. To use an old cliché, "the right hand must know what the left hand is doing."

An organizational chart improves on both job descriptions and the company handbook because it explains the relationship between managers and subordinates. The primary aim of an organizational chart is not to define the pecking order within the organization but to indicate the decision-making structure of the company.

Many contracting businesses are overwhelmed by paperwork. On any one project some or all of the following items may be needed:

▶ Contract for design work
▶ Formal design
▶ Design revision
▶ Cost estimate
▶ Contract/proposal for work to be done

▶ Work schedule

▶ Work order for crew

▶ Inventory/order materials

▶ Change orders

▶ Subcontractor contract(s)

▶ Bills from suppliers

▶ Profit/loss analysis

▶ Employee incentive payments

▶ Invoice sent to client

▶ Payment to suppliers and subcontractors

▶ Receipt from client

▶ Bank deposit

▶ Bank account reconciliation

Since it is highly unlikely that one department or one employee is responsible for all these tasks, it is paramount that each employee who handles a task understands who is responsible for the other tasks. Knowing the sequence of events and ensuring the proper flow of paperwork is the key to an efficient and productive office.

A variety of software programs now available feature organizational charts, making it simple to plug in names, tasks, and any other pertinent information. It also makes it easy to make changes as they arise . . . and they certainly do arise.

Because it is quite common to make changes during the course of a construction project, all employees must access the chart frequently. Mistakes once made are often hard to find and, if found, may be difficult to correct. A team approach to organizing and operating your company promotes efficiency and productivity, reduces errors, and creates a more functional organization. Using the right software can put you all on the same organizational page, literally. Hint: Try keeping your organizational chart on one page. Also, you should group people with the same title into one box to save space.

Lucid Chart (at www.lucidchart.com) can provide you with easy-to-create organizational charts at reasonable prices. A team of five, for example, would cost $20 per month total. SmartDraw (at www.smartdraw.com) is another good choice with some free downloads.

stat fact

Unsure about the value of incentives? Think again. Consumers are bombarded daily through the media with offers from merchants for "buy one get one free," "no payments for 12 months!" and "save 50 percent with coupon." It's a fact that incentives alter behavior. The trick for employers is to find the incentives that offer the biggest reward to the company at the least cost. Get to know your employees and think about what they want. Money is an obvious choice, but employers have also found that employees want group outings, parties, vacation days, and other perks.

Wrap-Up

▶ Managing employees can be a difficult and time-consuming endeavor.

▶ Writing an employee handbook is a great tool for both employer and employee.

▶ Both state and federal governments have rules and regulations regarding employment; understanding and following the rules will make an owner's job easier.

▶ Written job descriptions help employees understand their responsibilities and assist employers when reviewing employee performance.

▶ Caution when hiring minors: Stiff penalties apply if laws are violated.

▶ Wages are important, but benefits and incentives are vitally important to employee production.

▶ Reducing employee turnover saves money and increases productivity.

▶ An organizational chart is an excellent tool for improving communication. Look at some of the inexpensive organizational software options.

Errors and Omissions

Typically, successful entrepreneurs are eternal optimists. When presented with a challenge, they generally attack the problem without becoming discouraged. In fact, many consider difficult circumstances opportunities rather than setbacks—a minor detour instead of a train wreck. An excellent example of this is an excerpt from the movie *Apollo 13* (1995), which is based on the true story of the ill-fated manned mission to the moon:

> NASA Director: "This could be the worst disaster NASA's ever faced."

> Flight Director Gene Kranz: "With all due respect, sir, I believe this is gonna be our finest hour."

Failure Is Not an Option

The exact number of business failures among contracting companies is difficult to quantify, and it is even more difficult to know the reasons for failure. In fact, some business shutdowns may not even be classified as failures. In some cases the owner retires or sells the enterprise to another business. However, a general consensus is that roughly one half of all contracting businesses fail to survive more than five years, which is not unlike other businesses. Once they reach the five-year anniversary, however, chances for continued success are higher.

There isn't one single overriding reason why contracting businesses fail, but failures generally fall into several categories. We've touched on some in the course of this book, but it is a worthwhile exercise to review them. Most often, failure is not caused by a single factor but by several problems working together to sink a company. Among the most prevalent causes for business failures (listed in order of occurrence) are:

▶ *Very rapid growth not accompanied by a similar increase in resources.* If a business expands too quickly, it often cannot keep up with demand. Quality of work suffers because inexperienced or unskilled workers are hired and put to work with little or no training. Shortages of equipment also plague companies that grow too fast; when several work crews must share one piece of equipment, productivity and efficiency suffer, along with chances for profit.

▶ *Financial issues.* Improper budgeting and estimating, lack of cost controls, poor cash flow, and inadequate project management spell doom for many new businesses. Contractors must have more than creativity and technical skills to succeed in the competitive contracting environment.

▶ *Poor oversight and control at the upper management and project management levels.* When key staffers leave the company, they are often replaced by personnel who are either incapable of doing the work or are poorly trained. When the general economy is doing very well, the pool of skilled laborers shrinks, placing more strain on newer businesses.

▶ *Other factors beyond the control of the owner.* Economic downturns, high inflation, shortages of materials, or the dreaded "client from hell" can cause serious damage even when a contracting business seems to be running smoothly.

On the other hand, successful contractors share many similar characteristics. While there is no single formula for success, good contractors combine most of the following assets to establish an environment where success is expected, and usually achieved:

▶ Good training for new employees

▶ Good relationships with subcontractors

▶ Competitive wages and benefits with excellent incentives

▶ Low employee turnover

▶ Excellent management of financial resources and cash flow

▶ Cost controls

▶ Accurate job estimating

▶ Happy customers

▶ Happy employees and/or subcontractors

▶ Excellent communications with customers, employees, and subcontractors

▶ Hands-on project management

▶ Manageable debt

▶ Ability of owners and managers to identify potential problems before they get out of hand

▶ A cohesive and reasonable business plan

▶ Staying on top of changes in the industry from new rules and regulations to the latest in tools and technology.

tip ⓘ

Understanding how clients feel about your services is critical to success. One simple technique is to insert a short questionnaire with monthly invoices or post one on your website. Clients can rate the quality of your work, make written comments, and even request additional services. Making operational changes based on client input will not only help retain current clients, but will assist both sales and marketing efforts. If you are on Angie's List (which you can register to be listed at www.angieslist.com), you can look at reviews, as is also the case on Yelp (at www.yelp.com) and other ratings and review websites.

Client Complaints

Understanding exactly what angers clients the most about contractors and their services is an invaluable tool for owners. There are many resources available for owners to learn about the nature of client complaints. When a contractor understands the nature of a client, she is in a position to implement procedures to prevent trouble spots in the property development process.

Substandard workmanship is near the top of the list of client complaints. Clients expect the companies they hire to have skilled professionals, so if the work performed is unsatisfactory, trouble is right around the corner. Therefore, it is paramount that contractors properly train their employees and implement a good quality-control plan.

Often, contractors work inside a client's home, disrupting normal family life. These clients prepare for the "invasion" and become very agitated if the work does not begin as promised or takes much longer to complete than expected. Contractors can make life easier for all if they implement a reasonable scheduling system and teach their employees to be respectful of the client.

Little angers a client more than a contractor increasing the price of the project after work has been started. To avoid this problem, contractors must plan projects accurately so that all needed materials are accounted for. Designing a precise and accurate estimating system reduces errors as well. When it becomes necessary to make changes, the client must be informed in writing and must agree to both the physical alterations as well as changes in the cost of the project. Never change a rate without informing the client in advance that the cost may be higher than anticipated.

Most clients consider their homes to be their castles and are very proud of their ownership. Therefore, many of them become extremely upset when contractors do not clean up the job site both during the project and when work is completed. Failure to clean up a job site on a daily basis can give the client an impression that the contractor is performing shoddy work and does not take pride in what he does. While many people mention first impressions as an important factor when evaluating someone, the truth of the matter is that the final impression a contractor leaves when he or she finally departs the job site is more likely to be the dominant and lasting impression.

Clients pose all sorts of questions when choosing a contractor. Smart consumers talk to several contractors before engaging one to perform work. Contractors should be able to answer the following questions in a very timely manner. It should be noted, however, that clients

stat fact

Approximately two-thirds of home improvement clients cited a personal recommendation from a trusted friend as the key reason for hiring a contractor; about the same number of contractors believe that clients chose them because of the quality of their work or because of a referral from someone the client knew. This means you should always be leaving a business card or two or three with each customer.

appreciate it when a contractor or salesperson informs them that they do not know the answer but will get it within a day or two. Honesty is always the best policy. Be ready to answer:

▶ Are you licensed or registered in this state?

▶ Do you have adequate insurance coverage to protect my property and your employees?

▶ What other projects are you currently working on? (How's your schedule?)

▶ Can you provide references? I'd like to see some of the work you've done that is similar to the work I'm having done.

▶ Is your bid based on the same specifications as other bids?

▶ Do I need a building permit?

▶ How long do you estimate the job will take?

▶ Once you start on my project, will you stay on the job until it is completed?

▶ Do I have to make a decision right now? (The answer is always no.)

▶ Will you give me a written contract for the work you propose to do? (The answer is always yes.)

▶ Will you or someone else be doing the actual work?

▶ Who will be in charge of the project?

The Nightmare Client

While it is easy to find information and advice for consumers, much less is written about problem clients and how to deal with them. Some contractor associations offer advice, often through presentations at annual conferences, in their blogs, or even on their websites, about dealing with the problem client. When asked, most contractors will answer:

I do not like clients who

▶ continually ask for work to be redone, or continually change their minds;

▶ constantly complain and nitpick;

▶ don't pay on time, think you are their banker;

▶ try to get you to do more work at no additional charge;

▶ talk too much or watch you all the time.

Sometimes a contractor realizes that a potential client has a good chance to fall into the nightmare category. In this case, honesty is a good policy. Don't be afraid to say to the potential client, "No, thank you, we cannot do the work for you." However, some contractors simply raise their price in hope that the client will hire someone else. The

▶ Choose Carefully

When business is slow or the outlook for the economy as a whole is poor, competition among contractors can become intense. Competitors may drop their prices to levels below your break-even point. A contractor once commented, "Well, I'll take on some of these jobs because I can make it up on volume." Hogwash! It is silly to chase after these jobs because money lost on a project is gone forever. Another risk is actually agreeing to work for a nightmare client at a price just a few percentage points over your break-even point. Working with bad clients during tough times substantially increases the risk of losing money and certainly will result in anguish and unhappiness.

risks in this approach is that the unwanted client will agree to your price or you get the reputation that your prices are too high.

How to Handle Client Complaints

Few contracting jobs are 100 percent trouble free. Many times the problem, such as a weather delay, is not the fault of the contractor. However, all complaints must be addressed and dealt with carefully. The best rule of thumb is to approach every complaint with the attitude that the customer is always right (even if it's not true). There are some national department stores that have even accepted merchandise returns for products it does not even sell!

This approach does not always result in finding that the contractor is at fault. However, problem resolution must be the highest priority for a contracting company. Clients appreciate it when a contractor works with them instead of against them to resolve a dispute or misunderstanding. The following guidelines will help resolve complaints:

- ▶ Be courteous, and listen carefully to what the client has to say.
- ▶ Don't argue with the client.
- ▶ Do not make excuses.
- ▶ Resolve problems quickly.
- ▶ Remember the importance of good client relationships.
- ▶ Be reasonable even when the problem may not be your fault.
- ▶ Make written notes of discussions.

The ultimate goal should be to resolve disputes quickly and to the satisfaction of both parties. Contractors who stand behind their work even when they are not at fault reap huge rewards over the long term. Reputations are made by happy clients and additional profits are made from their recommendations of your business. This is not to say that a contractor should back down to the client's demand on each and every issue, but he must decide which battle is really worth fighting. If the marginal cost of resolving a problem is less than the expected long-term benefit, it makes good sense to spend the time or money to satisfy the client.

Remember, social media stretches far and wide, so people no longer just complain to their friend if they are unhappy with your services; they complain to thousands of readers at a time. Therefore, make customer service a very high priority.

Reliable Suppliers

The best-run businesses can be severely hurt by unreliable suppliers or subcontractors. When an entrepreneur has built a solid team, marketed its services successfully, implemented sound financial-planning procedures, and hired skilled and dedicated employees, he or she should be on the road to success. However, an efficient operation can become derailed if the materials needed to complete projects are not available when promised. The same is true when working with subcontractors: They must be reliable and complete their portion of the project both on time and within budget.

The best way to avoid problems with suppliers and subcontractors is to have an excellent communication system in place. While fax machines and email can facilitate the ordering process, we recommend that new business owners personally meet with their suppliers' representatives. By getting to know your salesperson, you'll be able to shortcut problems or bottlenecks and avoid unnecessary delays in the implementation of projects.

▶ Customers Can Help

TQM, or total quality management, is an approach to management that seeks to improve the quality of products and services by modifying services based on input from customers. The TQM process can be divided into four distinct categories: plan, do, check, and act. The first step is to gather data about a problem area, the second is to develop and implement a solution, the third is to verify the results by comparing before and after data, and the final step documents results and makes changes.

TQM was first used at manufacturing companies but is currently used in a wide variety of industries, including contracting.

The old adage "You get what you pay for" is often very true when considering which supplier to use or which subcontractor to hire. While your own work force might be top notch, your image will likely suffer if the materials or subcontractors you use are below average. You need to delve into the industry and do some research on suppliers in your area. Networking with other contractors, sometimes through associations, can be beneficial when getting some information about suppliers. Even as competitors you can both benefit either by ordering in greater quantity, which will be a bigger order for the supplier and may also result in a supplier offering you some better rates as a means of saying thank you for the referral. The contracting business is usually a small circle in most towns and even small cities.

Know the Enemy

"Competition is what kept me playing the psychological warfare of matching skill against skill, wit against wit."
—LOU BROCK, HALL OF FAME BASE STEALER FOR THE ST. LOUIS CARDINALS

Competition is good not only for the national economy but also for business. It forces business to eliminate waste and improve efficiency. The lifeblood of our free market, it rewards the most skilled businesses and weeds out the most inefficient. When poorly run businesses cease operations, consumers benefit because the overall quality of products and services improves; surviving businesses benefit because poorly run businesses place a drag on the entire industry, and once they are gone, its image can improve.

It is fairly easy to enter the contracting industry but much harder to rise above the crowd and dominate the market. One result of the relative ease of entry into contracting is that a segment of the industry is poorly managed, and a few bad apples can spoil the whole bushel. While some industries, and I'm sure you can name a few, have chronically poor reputations, a few others are always held in high regard, and the largest segment has a mixture. Contractors fall into this huge middle with plenty of rave reviews about some contractors countered with many complaints about contractors who did a poor job or took forever to complete a project.

Each entrepreneur should look at competition as a way to improve his organization's performance and success. Success is achieved by gathering better information about customers and new products than your competition, using that information for making the

stat fact

While entrepreneurs make up only about one-quarter of workers in the United States, they make up more than 60 percent of the millionaires.

best choices for your organization, and finally, turning the choices into actions that will provide a competitive advantage.

Never fear the competition. Never speak badly about the competition publicly. Just beat the competition with a better business plan, better financial management, better services and products, competitive pricing, and a reputation for doing good job.

As mentioned earlier, industry associations can benefit you as an entrepreneur. One excellent way to benefit from your competition is to join your local or regional industry association. Many of these groups schedule monthly meetings where members meet for dinner and listen to a speaker. It's not only an excellent time to learn about new initiatives in the industry but also a very good time to network with other owners and learn about their problems and successes. Supplier members usually attend these functions and can provide insight into new products or methods of installation. Associations also offer educational seminars during the year for both the business owner and key employees.

Employers who stand still, never changing their methods of operation, will eventually get run over by their competition. Skilled entrepreneurs are constantly on the alert for ways to improve all facets of their business. They use competition to improve their skills and help develop products and services that consumers value highly.

Hiring Subcontractors

In this era of specialization, the use of subcontractors has become very common. While there are many benefits to hiring a specialist to complete a portion of a property development project, caution is necessary. If the subcontractor is unqualified, the problems obviously offset the benefits. When hiring several subcontractors, the general contractor must have the ability to coordinate the work of these various individuals. In most projects, establishing a proper sequence of work is critical to success. The general contractor who hires the subcontractors must understand the responsibilities of each sub and how each fits into the overall construction sequence. For example, it is no use to schedule the asphalt contractor to install the driveway if the excavating contractor has not completed the rough grading.

Of foremost importance is hiring a subcontractor who is extremely reliable and able to meet the schedule established for the project. Because timing is usually crucial to a successful project, subcontractors must be able to complete their work in a timely manner. And because the best subcontractors are usually in great demand, a general contractor cannot risk losing the services of one sub because of the inefficiency of another. In addition, subcontractors must be able to meet the quality standards of the project set by the client, architect, and general contractor. While high-quality work is always expected of subcontractors, high-end projects with large budgets demand more skill and detail than low-budget projects. Subcontractors must understand what is expected of them and set their schedules accordingly.

An often-overlooked detail in hiring a subcontractor is insurance. When hiring a sub, the general contractor should be sure that the sub has proper insurance. While general liability insurance is very important, especially to protect against a lawsuit, carrying workers' compensation insurance is critical. Insurance companies usually audit their clients each year; during the audit, they verify that all subcontractors carry workers' compensation insurance. If they do not, then the general contractor will be charged an amount as if the subcontractors were employees of the company. It is not unusual for a general contractor to add 5 to 15 percent of the subcontractor's fee to the client's cost of the project, so an unexpected charge for workers' compensation insurance would nearly erase the profit generated by the subcontractor's work.

Wrap-Up

▶ Approximately 50 percent of new businesses fail to survive five years; however, once the fifth anniversary is reached, success is more likely.

▶ The primary complaint that clients have about contractors is substandard workmanship. Therefore, it is critical to hire quality employees and implement a good training program.

▶ Learn to recognize the warning signs of nightmare clients, and either decline to work for them or take extra precautions when preparing for the work.

▶ Because few projects are completely trouble free, learn how to handle client complaints in an understanding and professional manner.

▶ Reliable suppliers are extremely valuable.

▶ Competition can be very good for the best contractors.

▶ Hiring subcontractors can be beneficial, but care must be taken to hire the most skilled and reliable.

▶ Attention to detail is critical when working with clients, suppliers, and subcontractors.

11

PANIC
Is Proper

W ell, here we are at the final chapter, nearly ready to say goodbye. But instead of reaching an end, we hope this book will lead to a new beginning for you. While starting and running your own contracting business presents innumerable challenges and obstacles, the potential rewards, both personal and financial, far outweigh them. This chapter puts it all together, highlighting key points presented in the previous chapters.

When to PANIC

Often the daily life of a contractor is chaotic and messy. Schedules are disrupted by weather and absent employees. Projects are delayed because supplies are not available as promised. Clients call with change orders and seemingly inane concerns. Vendors call asking when payment will be made for merchandise. An employee thinks that his paycheck is incorrect. The computer crashes. A truck has a flat tire. Two work crews need the same piece of equipment. And your children are home from school because they have the flu, and your spouse has to tend to an ailing parent.

While many people would cower in fear or become completely unglued with crises, ending up reclining on a psychiatrist's couch, successful contractors and entrepreneurs thrive on activity, variety, and challenge. They are able to step back from daily chaos and view the big picture, understand where it is all leading, and forge ahead with the business of their business.

While successful contractors do not panic during challenging times, there are reasons why small-business owners should PANIC in order to be successful. While not inclusive or unique, the PANIC list gives the important factors required to become a thriving and happy contractor.

Astute readers will notice that we do not mention high intelligence or IQ, nor do we include advanced degrees. Intelligence and education are important, but they are not the most important aspect of becoming a successful contractor. Contractors are practical folks with unique talents that cannot be measured by university degrees and advanced-placement testing. Sure, they might have to pass competency tests in their home state, but these are usually practical exercises devised by politicians attempting to protect the public.

Let's PANIC Now

Of course, entrepreneurs should not actually panic when events take a wrong turn; just remember that failure is not an option. However, after reading the remainder of the chapter you'll understand that the definition of PANIC cannot be found in any dictionary.

P Is for Perseverance

Successful contractors exhibit steady persistence in spite of the many obstacles that they meet each day. Running a business is a difficult, sometimes discouraging, undertaking.

Entrepreneurs are able to look to the distant future, stick with their long-range plan, and not get sidetracked by temporary difficulties. Perseverance implies a great deal of optimism about the future and a strong passion for your work. If you really believe in the future and believe that your work is important to your community, you'll be able to overcome adversity, win clients, and own a respected, profitable, and successful business. And having faith in yourself allows you to go further than others and rise to the top of your profession.

A Is for Accounting

A good sense of financial management is critical to succeeding as an entrepreneur. Because cash flow is the lifeblood of most businesses, including those in the contracting industry, timely management of income and expenses often makes the difference between a successful business and one that ultimately fails.

In many parts of the country, contractors have to contend with seasonal fluctuations of income and expenses, which makes long-range financial planning essential for success. Successful contractors establish a reasonable budget, use it to implement a competitive system for establishing prices, and regularly monitor both income and expenses to ensure that their financial management plan is on track.

Starting your own contracting business involves a certain amount of risk because of the degree of competition in the industry and because many specialty contractors require a substantial financial investment just to get started. However, the risks can be greatly reduced by employing a sound and consistent financial plan.

N Is for Natural Ability

In general, contractors are creative craftspeople who use their innate skills to develop their business. Creativity comes in many forms: Some have the power of visualization and can "see" how the many elements of

tip

Typically, a landscape contractor who works in the northern part of the country may have to lay off the majority of his employees for three months during the winter. Income drops to a trickle, but fixed costs need to be paid. Before any bonuses are paid to key executives, he ensures that enough cash is on hand to tide the company through the lean months. As one of the owners told us, "In the winter it often seems like we dig a big hole in the ground and throw money into it." He also has a mathematical formula for distributing bonuses that ensures there are funds available to reinvest in the company as it grows. Not only is the company able to purchase new equipment, it keeps its interest expenses at a manageable level.

a project fit together. Others are masters of scale and proportion who can place individual elements together. Yet others are true artists who can make perfect individual elements that fit into the whole. Many have an excellent aesthetic sense and make creations that have good taste and a sense of beauty. Finally, successful contractors understand that many times "form follows function," and they use their skills to ensure that their creations not only look appropriate for their task but also "work." Whatever form or forms of creativity these entrepreneurs display, they all have full confidence in their own natural abilities. This self-confidence allows them to forge ahead and take on the risks that are inherent in starting a new business.

Natural ability and creativity are not limited to merely the physical aspect of a contractor's work. Creative accounting can save a contracting company thousands of dollars each year. Creative use of employee incentives can raise the level and quality of the work produced by the company. Every aspect of managing a contracting business can benefit from creative thought, and the most successful entrepreneurs tap into their own natural abilities. In addition, contractor-owners must be able to multitask, that is, understand, recognize, and react to all that is happening around them—not only the day-to-day events of running the business but also the consequences of many conflicting personalities working together for a common goal. On the other hand, owners must be able to focus on the immediate task at hand and avoid getting sidetracked on unimportant issues.

▶ College Drop-Outs

While we applaud those who aspire to higher education and do not recommend dropping out of college, several famous entrepreneurs actually did drop out of college (or took a leave of absence) to pursue their dreams. Their natural abilities and creativity allowed them to succeed without completing their formal education. Here's a short list of well-known names with the company they founded and the college they attended: Bill Gates, Microsoft, Harvard; Michael Dell, Dell Computer, University of Texas; Steve Jobs, Apple, Inc., Reed College; Paul Allen, Microsoft, Washington State University; and Mark Zuckerberg, Facebook, Harvard.

At the other end of the spectrum, Google, Inc.'s founders Larry Page and Sergey Bin both received master's degrees from Stanford; in fact, seven of the top-ten CEOs of U.S. companies, including Warren Buffet, have college degrees. Several have master's degrees, and one has a Ph.D.

I Is for Instinct

Most of the skills required to operate a successful contracting business can be learned, either through formal training or from experience. However, instinct, which really means having a good feel for business, is something that cannot be taught. It is the intangible something that separates the most successful entrepreneurs from the average business owner. Those with good instincts really know themselves and, most importantly, understand their own strengths and weaknesses, turning this knowledge into an asset, and creating an efficient and profitable entity. These folks not only have the ability to talk a good game, they can also execute their plans to the benefit of the company.

Business owners who really understand themselves also understand their own shortcomings and take steps to balance their weaknesses by surrounding themselves with people who compensate for them. The best and most successful realize that their success is often a result of the people around them rather than themselves alone. Instinct, or good business sense, allows these entrepreneurs to get the most out of the people around them and build a true team with a common goal.

Confidence is an asset, arrogance a liability.

C Is for Communication

Excellent communication skills make up the final section of my definition of the word PANIC. Communicating is less about making stirring speeches than it is about the ability to convey enthusiasm and energy to both employees and clients. With the emergence of the internet, email, cellphones, and voicemail, we have become more impersonal than at any time in recent memory. Thus, in the modern world, possessing good people skills is of greater importance to the entrepreneur. Not only must the contractor be able to accurately share his or her corporate vision to fellow workers but he or she must also be able to convey enthusiasm, professionalism, and sincerity to clients.

Communicating with employees starts with hiring the right people for the job. Good hiring is a result of being able to put yourself in another person's shoes and see what they see, feel what they feel, and have sensitivity to their expectations. Upon hiring the right people, good communication means having the ability to motivate the new employees to succeed beyond their dreams, pushing them to their creative limits, and then recognizing their achievements. It also means respecting and utilizing the knowledge, wisdom, and practical experiences of the seasoned employees.

Communicating with clients follows a similar path. The ability to sell your service or product requires that you be able to sit in their chairs, understand their problems, and focus on their dreams.

It's imperative that you remember good communication is not only about what you have to say or how enthusiastic you are, it is very much about how well you listen.

But, What If . . .?

Not every entrepreneur possesses all of the traits mentioned in PANIC. Not everyone is a good communicator, not all have excellent natural ability. But to succeed, you must recognize both your strengths and weaknesses. When you do this, you will have the ability to hire people who are strong in areas you are weak. The combination of talent within a company creates a stronger and more powerful entity.

Put Me in, Coach

With all due respect to professional baseball, professional basketball, and NASCAR fans, most polls indicate that professional football holds the top spot as America's favorite sport. Football is a very complex business requiring the expertise of dozens of people in each organization. Gone are the days of Vince Lombardi and George Halas who controlled entire football operations with only a handful of assistants. Today, most teams separate the head coach and general manager positions, and it is not unusual to have 16 or 17 assistant coaches on the staff. The salary cap and player contracts are so complex that only a team of lawyers can understand them. Running a business is much like coaching a football team. The head football coach oversees both the offense and the defense; assistants manage the details of each. In order to win, both offense and defense have to play extremely well.

The offensive squad of a business includes the marketing department, sales force, and the bidding and estimating departments. Depending on the size of the company, landing a $40,000 or $200,000 job can be compared to a quarterback throwing a long touchdown pass; but the business "offense" still needs to book $500 and $5,000 jobs, just like the offense needs to gain a few yards at a time to get a first down. For the business, the "defense" is made up of those who manage the finances of the company. If they are not successful, the game gets out of hand, and success (victory) is impossible. A football team may have an excellent offense, but if its defense is weak, it will likely lose more games than it wins. Likewise, you may have many jobs and plenty of income, but you may not be playing defense and protecting that income. A team may score 35 points, but if they give up 40 points, they lose. If you bring in $1.2 million and spend $1.8 million, you will also lose.

Just as teams may have a few losing season, so will you, but you can only last so long in businesses without winning. That's why you need to have both offense and defense, making money and protecting enough money that you show a profit.

If you are not sure how this works then go back and read Chapter 7, study contribution margin, and understand what the offense must do if the defense overspends the budget.

Just consider recent winners of the Super Bowl, football's world championship contest. They have almost always had the better defense. Look at many of the great teams of their day—the Packers, Steelers, 49ers, and more recently the Denver Broncos; even though they had great quarterbacks like Brett Favre, Ben Rothlisberger, and Payton Manning , they featured exceptional defensive teams. And they all won lots of games—and Super Bowls.

Release all your creativity and passion with your offensive plan, but be stubborn and watchful with your defensive scheme. Teamwork wins when players on both sides of the ball do their part.

The Beginning

As this book concludes, your new life begins.

"The important thing is not being afraid to take a chance. Remember, the greatest failure is to not try. Once you find something you love to do, be the best doing it."
—DEBBI FIELDS, FOUNDER OF MRS. FIELDS COOKIES

Construction Contracting Resources

They say you can never be rich enough or young enough. While these could be argued, we believe you can never have enough resources. Therefore, we present for your consideration a wealth of sources for you to check into, check out, and harness for your own personal information blitz.

These sources are tidbits, ideas to get you started on your research. They are by no means the only sources out there, and they should not be taken as the ultimate answer. Research has been done on each company, but businesses do tend to move, change, fold, and expand. Please do your homework carefully, and then get out and start investigating.

Books

Architectural Graphic Standards for Residential Construction by American Institute of Architects, Nina M. Giglio and Dennis Hall (Wiley, 2010).

Common Sense Economics: What Everyone Should Know About Wealth and Prosperity by James Gwartney, Richard Stroup, and Dwight Lee (St. Martin Press, 2005).

DeWALT Construction Estimating Complete Handbook (DEWALT Series) by Adam Ding and the American Contractors Educational Services (DEWALT, 2016).

The General Contractor: How to Be a Great Success or Failure by Joe Egan (Egan Publications, 2012).

The Only Three Questions That Still Count: Investing by Knowing What Others Don't by Ken Fisher (Wiley, 2012).

Running a Successful Construction Company by David Gerstel (Taunton Press, 2002).

Start Your Own Business by The Staff of Entrepreneur Media, Inc. (Entrepreneur Press, 2015).

Construction, Remodeling, and General Contractor Magazine Websites

Constructor, www.constructormagazine.com

Engineering News-Record, www.enr.com

Free Trade Magazines, www.freetrademagazines.com

Modern Contractor Solutions, www.mcsmag.com

Remodeling, www.remodeling.hw.net

LinkedIn (www.linkedin.com) Group

Associated General Contractors, subcontractors, www.linkedin.com/groups/1930563/profile

Government Resources

U.S. Equal Employment Opportunity Commission—(800) 669-4000, www.eeoc.gov

Business U.S.A.—For general information, (844) BIZ-USA2, http://business.usa.gov

Internal Revenue Service—(800) 829-4933, www.irs.gov

Small Business Administration—(800) 827-5722, www.sba.gov

U.S. Department of Labor—(866) 487-2365, www.dol.gov

Workers' Compensation—(866) 927-2667, www.workerscompensation.com

U.S. Department of Transportation—(855) 368-4200, www.transportation.gov

General Business Websites

Bankrate, www.bankrate.com

Bloomberg Business, www.bloomberg.com

CNN Money, http://money.cnn.com

Entrepreneur, https://www.entrepreneur.com/

MarketWatch, www.marketwatch.com

Microsoft Service Network, www.msn.com

The Wall Street Journal, www.WSJ.com

Cellphone Information

My Rate Plan, www.myrateplan.com

Phone Scoop, www.phonescoop.com

PC magazine cell-phone reviews, www.pcmag.com/reviews/cell-phones

PhoneArena, www.phonearena.com

Contractor Resources

Websites 4 Contractors, www.websites4contractors.com

Contractor Talk—Professional Construction & Remodeling Forum plus blogs articles and product reviews, www.contractortalk.com

Listings and Places to Post Your Services

Angie's List, www.angieslist.com

Serquest, http://serquest.com

The Good Contractors List, http://thegoodcontractorslist.com

1 800 Contractor, www.1800contractor.com

Accounting Software

Sage One, www.sageone.com

AccounEedge Pro, www.accountedge.com

FreshBooks, www.freshbooks.com

QuickBooks Pro, http://quickbooks.intuit.com

Find Your Credit Rating

Annual Credit Report—"The only source for your free credit reports." Authorized by
federal law, www.annualcreditreport.com.

Credit Rating Bureaus

Equifax
P.O. Box 740241
Atlanta, GA 30374
(800) 685-1111
www.equifax.com

Experian
P.O. Box 9554
Allen, TX 75013
(888) 397-3742
www.experian.com

TransUnion LLC
P.O. Box 1000
Chester, PA 19022

(800) 888-4213

www.transunion.com

Education/Industry Links

College Board—website to search for colleges and universities (www.collegeboard.org)

Architecture

The National Architectural Accrediting Board, http://naab.org/home

American Institute of Architects, http://aia.org/

Society of Landscape Architecture, https://asla.org

Engineering

ABET, www.abet.org

American Society for Engineering Education, www.asee.org

National Society of Professional Engineers, www.nspe.org

Design-Build Institute of America, www.dbia.org

Construction Industry Associations

The Blue Book of Building and Construction, http://thebluebook.com/links.html

The Home Improvement Web, https://www.homeimprovementweb.com/directory/
    Contractors/Associations/

Information and Tools

Counselors to America's Small Business, www.score.org

StartupBiz, www.startupbiz.com

Social Media

www.facebook.com

https://twitter.com

www.linkedin.com

www.pinterest.com

www.tumblr.com

www.instagram.com

www.flickr.com

Social Media Management

Hootsuite, www.hootsuite.com

VerticalResponse, www.verticalresponse.com

Sprout Social, http://sproutsocial.com

Sendible, http://sendible.com

Glossary

Accrual accounting. An accounting system that recognizes revenue when earned and expenses when incurred; income and expenses are recorded at the end of an accounting period even though cash has not been received or paid.

Break-even. The point where expenses and income are equal.

Business plan. A written summary of how a business intends to organize an entrepreneurial endeavor and implement activities and procedures necessary and sufficient for the business to succeed.

Cash accounting. An accounting method that recognizes revenue and expenses when cash is actually received or disbursed rather than when earned or incurred.

Cash flow. An accounting term that refers to the amount of cash that is received and spent by a business; it is not a measure of profitability; a profitable company can fail because of problems with cash flow.

Contribution margin. The amount of revenue available to pay fixed costs and profits after paying direct costs and variable costs.

Debt financing. A method of financing a business that relies on borrowing to fund the initial activities of the business.

Demographics. The statistical characteristics of a population typically utilized in business to establish a defined customer base to which to market goods and/or services.

Design/build. Generally, a contracting company that provides both professional design services and construction services; most often these are bundled into one package.

Direct costs. Expenses directly related to specific jobs or projects; usually includes materials, labor, and labor burden and may include the cost of equipment rental and subcontractors.

Employee handbook. A guide detailing the rules, regulations, guidelines, and acceptable manner of conduct within a company as well as the penalties for failure to comply.

Equity financing. A method of financing an enterprise in which a company sells stock; individuals who purchase the stock have ownership interest in the company.

Fixed costs. An expense that remains constant regardless of a change in the level of a company's business or income.

General contractor. A contractor who does construction on a building or works on other home or property improvements for clients; may have his or her own work force or may hire independent subcontractors.

Labor burden. Costs of labor in addition to wage or salary; includes payroll taxes, insurance, and other associated expenses.

Lien. A legal claim on a piece of property used to ensure payment of a debt or obligation.

Marginalism. An economic concept used to determine if an additional expense will result in a benefit greater than the additional cost.

Marketing. The action or business of promoting products or services to a mass or specific audience. Market research and advertising are included.

Mission statement. A written statement that summarizes the purpose of a business.

SDS (Safety Data Sheets) or MSDS (Material Safety Data Sheet). Both are important features of workplace safety. Both sheets provide information on dealing with toxic or hazardous materials. Businesses are required to maintain a current file of these sheets as applicable to their enterprise.

OJT (On the Job Training). Learning a trade or job without formal education by hands-on involvement.

OSHA (Occupational Health and Safety Administration). A branch of the federal government responsible for establishing and enforcing procedures to prevent workplace injuries.

Overhead. Fixed costs plus variable costs.

PBX (Private Branch Exchange). A computerized telephone system that can handle many calls, both incoming and outgoing, at the same time; voice mail and call forwarding are popular additional features.

Social Media. The use of websites and applications for users to connect with one another to network and share content and information.

Subcontractor: An independent contractor who takes jobs from the principal contractor or from another subcontractor.

TQM (Total Quality Management). A management strategy aimed at creating awareness of quality in all organizational processes; provides a system under which everyone in the organization can strive for customer satisfaction.

Workers' compensation insurance. Insurance that is designed to protect the earnings of employees who are injured or become ill as a result of their work; premium costs are based on payroll.

Index

A

About Us pages, 99
accountants, 37, 38–39, 45, 85, 89
accounting, 38–39, 85, 89, 131.
    See also budgeting; financial
    management
accounting tools, 65–66
accrual accounting, 38–39, 89
actual value insurance, 40
advertising, 76, 103–104. *See also*
    marketing
advisors, 27, 36, 37, 38–39, 45
angel investors, 31
Angie's List, 101, 121
answering machines, 52
architects, 4, 9, 10, 11, 53
assets, return on, 85
association memberships, 105
attention to detail, 58
attorneys, 36, 39, 45
audits, 44–45, 128

B

backlinks, 100
backup media, 53
bank accounts, 57
bank payments, 73
bankers, 31, 39. *See also* debt
    financing
benefits, employee, 112–115
big picture viewpoint, 9–10, 58
bonuses, 114
break-even analysis, 28, 91
break-even point, 80, 85, 88,
    90–91
budget analysis, 91–94
budgeting. *See also* financial
    management
    assistance and tools for, 64–66
    break-even point in, 80, 85,
        88, 90–91
    contribution margin
        calculations in, 88–91, 135

direct cost projections, 67–72, 75, 78, 80, 89

estimates and, 80–83

fixed cost projections, 72–75, 78, 80, 89, 131

overhead projections, 77–80, 84

profit and, 84–85, 88–90

purpose of, 66, 131

revenues vs.spending in, 66–67

variable cost projections, 75–77

business plan software, 29–30

business plans, 25–30, 39. *See also* financing

business structures, 36–38

C

C corporations, 37, 38

capital, return on, 85

capital equipment funds, 73

cash accounting, 38–39

cash flow, 18–19, 28, 32, 56–57, 73, 107, 131

cash payments, 57

cell phones, 51–52

certification classes, 114–115

change orders, 5

character traits and skills for success, 9–10, 12–14, 19–22, 57–60, 121, 130–135

checking accounts, 57

client complaints, 121–125

communication skills, 20–21, 133–134

communication systems, 50–52

community health and welfare, 8

community-based websites, advertising on, 104

company vehicles, 113–114

competition, 26, 124, 126

complaints, 121–125

computers, 52–53

confidence, 133

construction liens, 56

construction tools and equipment, 16–17, 55, 76

contact pages, 100

continuing education opportunities, 15–16, 114–115

contractors vs. employees, 41–42

contribution margin, 88–91, 135

copy machines, 52

corporations, 37, 38

cost efficiency, 84

costs

direct, 67–72, 75, 78, 80, 89

fixed, 72–75, 78, 80, 89, 131

labor. *See* labor burden

variable, 75–77

creativity, 132

credibility, 102, 105

credit, buying on, 18–19, 56

credit cards, 56

credit ratings, 18–19

credit unions, 31–32

customer complaints, 121–125

customer demographics, 27, 103, 105

customer service, 51, 121–125, 134

D

data storage, 53

debt financing, 31–33, 39, 73

delegating, 21–22

demographics, 27, 103, 105

depreciation, 76

design/build contracting companies, 4–5

detail, attention to, 58

differentiation, 26

difficult clients, 123–124

direct costs, 67–72, 75, 78, 80, 89

disciplining employees, 114

documentation, 43

domain names, 104

E

earnings statements, 28

economic importance of contracting industry, 5–6

educational opportunities, 9, 11, 15–16, 114–115

employee handbooks, 110–111
employees
    applications and hiring forms, 111
    bonuses and incentives, 77, 114, 117
    communicating with, 20–21, 133–134
    contractors vs., 41–42
    managing, 19–20, 59, 109–110
    minors, 56, 112
    payroll records, 45
    payroll taxes, 68–70
    performance records, 44
    retaining, 115–116
    training, 11–12, 59–60, 106, 122
    wages and benefits, 42–43, 112–115
Employer Identification Number (EIN), 40
employment taxes, 68–70
engineering requirements, 11
equipment and tools, 16–17, 50–55, 76
equity, return on, 85
equity financing, 30–31
estimates, 80–83
executive summaries, 26
expense and revenue tracking, 91–95
expert status, 102

F

failure, causes of, 120–121
fax machines, 52
federal rules and regulations, 40–41, 55–56
field labor costs, 67–71, 94–95
financial management, 28, 38–39, 63–66, 85, 89, 91–95, 120, 131. *See also* budgeting
financial planning, 131
financial statements, 28
financing, 17–18, 19, 30–33, 39, 73
fixed costs, 72–75, 78, 80, 89, 131
flexibility, 58–59
fliers, 104
friends and relatives as financing source, 30
funding, 17–18, 19, 30–33, 39

G

general contractors, 2, 5, 127–128

general liability insurance, 70, 128
government rules and regulations, 40–42, 55–56
growth, 106–107, 120
guest blogging, 102

H

health considerations, 13
health insurance, 43, 70–71
hiring employees. *See* employees
home offices, 48–49
homepages, 99

I

incentive plans, 114, 117
incentives, employee, 77
income potential, 84
income statements, 28
income taxes, 45
incorporating, 37, 38
independent contractors, 2. *See also* subcontractors
inland marine insurance, 40
inside contractors, 3
instinct, 133
insurance, 39–40
internet access, 53

J

job applications, 111
job descriptions, 111–112

L

labor burden
    break-even point and, 80
    in estimates, 80–83
    field labor costs, 67–71
    office staff costs, 72–74
    in overhead calculations, 78–80
    in variable costs, 76–77
labor law posters, 55
landscape architects, 4, 9, 10, 11
lawyers, 36, 39, 45

legal business structures, 36–38
liability insurance, 70, 128
liens, 56
lifestyle considerations, 9, 59
limited liability companies (LLC), 36–37, 38
links on websites, 100, 101
loans, 31–33, 39, 73. *See also* financing
locating your business, 48–49
logos, 97–98
LucidChart organizational chart software, 117

M

management expertise, 19–22, 59, 103–110
management teams, 27
managing people, 19–20, 59, 109–110
marginalism, 66
marketing
    advertising, 76, 103–104
    customer demographics and, 27, 103, 105
    definition of, 98
    expert status and, 102
    guest blogging, 102
    logos, 97–98
    preparing for growth and, 106–107
    press releases, 102–103
    print advertising, 103–104
    publicity, 99–100, 102
    self-promotion, 102–103
    social media presence, 101–102, 103
    sponsoring local sports teams, 104
    websites, 98–101
    word of mouth, 105–106
    writing articles, 102
marketing plans, 26–27
Material Safety Data Sheet (MSDS), 55–56
math terms, 87–88
mechanic's liens, 56
Medicare taxes, 68
menu ads, 104
minors, employing, 56, 112
mission statements, 30

mobile phones, 51–52
money market accounts, 57
monitoring expenses and revenues, 91–95
MSDS (Material Safety Data Sheet), 55–56
multi-function machines, 52

N

naming your business, 104
natural ability, 131–132
negative feedback, 121–125
nest eggs for personal expenses, 17–18
net income, 84–85
newspaper ads, 104
nightmare clients, 123–124

O

Occupational Health and Safety Administration (OSHA), 4, 55
office equipment, 50–55
office space, 49–50, 73
office staff, 72–74
office supplies, 53–55
off-season services, 60
online data storage, 53
online offers, 100
online presence, 98–103, 121, 125
on-the-job training (OJT), 11–12
organizational charts, 116–117
organizational skills, 21, 59
OSHA (Occupational Health and Safety Administration), 4, 55
outside contractors, 4
outsourcing payroll processing, 116
overhead, 77–80, 84
overtime costs, 71

P

paid vacations and holidays, 70, 113
PANIC list, 130–134
partnerships, 36, 38
payroll processing, 116
payroll records, 45
payroll taxes, 68–70

PBX telephone system, 50–51
people management, 19–20, 59, 109–110
perseverance, 130–131
persistence, 131
personal finances, 30
phone directory ads, 103
physical and mental health, 13
placemat ads, 104
position descriptions, 111–112
press, 99–100
press releases, 102–103
price fixing, 76
pricing, 27, 63–64, 75, 76, 84–85
print advertising, 103–104
private branch exchange (PBX) telephone
    system, 50–51
professional associations, 105
profit, 84–85, 88–90
profit and loss statements (P&L), 28
promoting you business. *See* marketing
property development contractors, 2–5, 8
property owners as general contractors, 5
publicity, 99–100, 102

R
rapid growth pitfalls, 106–107, 120
record keeping, 42, 43–45, 53, 57, 64, 113–
    114
relatives and friends as financing source, 30
replacement cost insurance, 40
requirements for professional fields, 10–11
retaining employees, 115–116
retirement plans, 113
revenue and expense tracking, 91–95
revenues vs.spending, 66–67
reviews on social media sites, 103, 121
risk planning, 28
rules and regulations, 55–56

S
S corporations, 37, 38
safety, 8

safety considerations in construction, 8
sales per labor dollar, 75–77, 94–95
savings accounts, 57
SBA loans, 32–33
scheduling, 5, 59
seasonality of the construction business, 60
self-confidence, 13, 133
self-promotion, 102–103
skills and traits for success, 9–10, 12–14,
    19–22, 57–60, 121, 130–135
Small Business Association (SBA) loans,
    32–33
small business tax credits, 43
SmartDraw organizational chart software,
    117
smartphones, 51–52
social media presence, 101–102, 103, 121, 125
social security taxes, 68
software upgrades, 64
sole proprietorship, 36, 37–38
specialty trade contractors, 4
spending vs. revenues, 66–67
sponsoring local sports teams, 104
spreadsheets, 64–65
starting a construction business
    customer loyalty and, 6
    finding a niche, 6
    funding a startup, 17–18
    having the right tools, 16–17, 55
    health considerations, 13
    lifestyle considerations, 9, 59
    skills and traits needed, 9–10, 12–14,
        19–22, 57–60, 121, 130–135
    typical day in the business, 58–59
    understanding contracting lingo, 17
startup funds, 17–18
state rules and regulations, 40–41
storage space, 50
subcontractors, 2–5, 41–42, 68, 125–126,
    127–128
successful contractors, traits and skills of,
    9–10, 12–14, 19–22, 57–60, 121, 130–135

supplier credit, 56–57
suppliers, 125–126

T

tablets, 52–53
tax credits, 43
tax deductions, 44
taxes, 35–36, 40–41, 43–44, 45, 89
team sponsorship as advertising, 104
telephone answering machines, 52
telephone systems, 50–51
time management, 13–14
tools and equipment, 16–17, 55, 76
Total Quality Management (TQM), 125
tracking expenses and revenues, 91–95
traits and skills for success, 9–10, 12–14,
    19–22, 57–60, 121, 130–135
travel expenses, 75–76
tuition assistance, 114–115
turnkey construction operations, 2
turnover, employee, 115–116

U

unemployment taxes, 68–70

V

variable costs, 75–77
vehicles, 55, 113–114
venture capitalists, 30–31

W

wages and benefits, 112–115
website builder sites, 100
websites, 98–101
word of mouth, 105–106
work spaces, 49–50
workers' compensation insurance, 44–45, 70,
    73, 115, 128
written warnings to employees, 114

Y

Yelp.com, 101, 121